ON BEING BLUE

A PHILOSOPHICAL INQUIRY

ON BEING BLUE

❧

WILLIAM GASS

DAVID R. GODINE · BOSTON

David R. Godine, Publisher
306 DARTMOUTH STREET, BOSTON, MASSACHUSETTS

ISBN 0-87923-183-1 (trade)
ISBN 0-87923-190-4 (deluxe)
ISBN 0-87923-237-4 (softcover)
LCC NO. 75-43013

THIRD PRINTING

PRINTED IN THE UNITED STATES OF AMERICA

I

BLUE pencils, blue noses, blue movies, laws, blue legs and stockings, the language of birds, bees, and flowers as sung by longshoremen, that lead-like look the skin has when affected by cold, contusion, sickness, fear; the rotten rum or gin they call blue ruin and the blue devils of its delirium; Russian cats and oysters, a withheld or imprisoned breath, the blue they say that diamonds have, deep holes in the ocean and the blazers which English athletes earn that gentlemen may wear; afflictions of the spirit—dumps, mopes, Mondays—all that's dismal—low-down gloomy music, Nova Scotians, cyanosis, hair rinse, bluing, bleach; the rare blue dahlia like that blue moon shrewd things happen only once in, or the call for trumps in whist (but who remembers whist or what the death of unplayed games is like?), and correspondingly the flag, Blue Peter, which is our signal for getting under way; a swift pitch, Confederate money, the shaded slopes of clouds and mountains, and so the constantly increasing absentness of Heaven (*ins Blaue hinein,* the Germans say), consequently the color of everything that's empty: blue bottles, bank accounts, and compliments, for instance, or, when the sky's turned turtle, the blue-green bleat of ocean (both the same), and, when in Hell, its neatly landscaped rows of concrete huts and gas-blue flames; social registers, examination booklets, blue bloods, balls, and bonnets, beards, coats, collars, chips, and cheese . . . the pedantic, indecent and censorious . . . watered twilight, sour sea: through a scrambling of accidents, blue has become their color, just as it's stood for fidelity. Blue laws took their hue from the paper they were printed on. Blue noses were named for a potato. E. Haldeman-Julius' little library, where I first read Ellen Key's *Evolution of Love*, vainly hoping for a cock stand, had such covers. In the same series, which sold for a dime in those days, were the love letters of that Portuguese nun, Mariana Alcoforado, an overwrought and burdensome lady, certainly, whose existence I callously forgot until I read of her again in Rilke.

The first of these pocket pamphlets was, inevitably, the *Rubáiyát*. It had the right sentiments. It was the right length. It came in pretty quatrains. And like a pair of polished shoes, it had just the right world-weariness and erotic sheen. No. 19, the nearest I got to The Jug and Bough, was entitled, *Nietzsche: Who He Was and What He Stood For*, by M. A. Mugge, Ph.D. All those capitals were formerly for God. There was another, I remember, that reproduced the wartime speeches of Woodrow Wilson in a type which sometimes sagged toward the bottom of the page as though weakened by the weight of the words above. The blue of these books is pale by now, the paper brittle as communion bread, while my association of Wilde and Darrow with the color, once so intense, has faded too. My cock did not stand for Nietzsche either, nor did Mrs. Annie Besant's essay on the future

[4]

of marriage cause a stir. One had to go to Liveright for that—to other colors: Black and Gold—where you could be warmed by Stendhal, Huneker, and Jules Romain, by Balzac and Remy de Gourmont, and where the decadence of Pierre Louys was genuine and not a bit of blueness dripped on scarcely curdled cheese.

John Middleton Murry edited *The Blue Review* for the three distinguished issues of its life, and something called *The Blue Calendar* predicted the weather from 1895 to 1898 without ever being right. Only a nickel, also blue, out of the same dry attic box, *The Bibelot*, a Lilliputian periodical with a Gothically lettered cover which fairly cried out ART, rose into my unhealthy hands. It came down from Maine instead of in from Kansas, and reprinted pieces that had previously vanished in the pages of *The Dark Blue*, a vague Pre-Raphaelite monthly with a title as frustratingly incomplete as a broken musical phrase. These rhapsodies went into print and out of sight the way trout, I'm sure, still disappear among the iridescences of my childhood Ohio's cold, bottomless Blue Hole, suddenly to emerge again in the clear, swift streams and shallow ponds it feeds as if nothing magical had happened to them. Each of the magazine's meager issues featured a single, slightly sacred, faintly wicked, and always delicately perfumed work by William Morris or Francis Thompson, Andrew Lang or others. The set I saw concluded quietly with Swinburne's tribute to the painter Simeon Solomon (even then in bluish oblivion). Now this fading poet's forgotten essay furnishes us with our first example, before we are quite ready for any: the description of two figures in a painting . . . the prose of a shade of blue I leave to you.

One girl, white-robed and radiant as white water-flowers, has half let fall the rose that droops in her hand, dropping leaf by leaf like tears; both have the languor and the fruitful air of flowers in a sultry place; their leaning limbs and fervent faces are full of the goddess; their lips and eyes allure and await the invisible attendant Loves. The clear pearl-white cheeks and tender mouths have still about them the subtle purity of sleep; the whole drawing has upon it the heavy incumbent light of summer but half awake. Nothing of more simple and brilliant beauty has been done of late years.

Lang, plainly fond of the color, edited *The Blue Poetry Book*. From her window Katherine Mansfield sees a garden full of wallflowers and blue enamel saucepans, and sets the observation down in a letter to Frieda Lawrence she'll never mail. Stephen Crane wrote and posted *The Blue Hotel*, Malcolm Cowley *Blue Juniata*, and Conrad Aiken *Blue Voyage*. Like rainwater and white chickens, KM exclaims:

> Very beautiful, O God! is a blue tea-pot with two white cups attending; a red apple among oranges addeth fire to flame—in the white book-cases the books fly up and down in scales of colour, with pink and lilac notes recurring, until nothing remains but them, sounding over and over.

Then there is the cold Canadian climate and the color of deep ice. The gill of a fish. Lush grass. The whale. Jay. Ribbon. Fin.

*   *   *

Among the derivations of the word, I especially like *blavus*, from medieval Latin, and the earlier, more classical, *flavus*, for the discolorations of a bruise, so that it sometimes meant yellow, with perhaps a hint of green beneath the skin like naughty underclothes. Once, one blushed blue, though to blush like a blue dog, as the cliché went then, was not to blush at all. Covenanters, against royal red, flaunted it. They were true blue, they said.

[6]

And Boswell tells us, out of his blue life, that Benjamin Stilling-
fleet wore blue wool undress hose to Elizabeth Montague's literary tea-at-homes. Perhaps to Elizabeth Carter's too. And even
Hannah More's.

> BLUE.—Few words enter more largely into the composition of slang,
> and colloquialisms bordering on slang, than does the word BLUE. Ex-
> pressive alike of the utmost contempt, as of all that men hold dear-
> est and love best, its manifold combinations, in ever varying shades
> of meaning, greet the philologist at every turn. A very Proteus, it
> defies all attempts to trace the why and wherefore of many of the
> turns of expression of which it forms a part. . . .
> (Farmer and Henley: *Slang and Its Analogues*)

So a random set of meanings has softly gathered around the
word the way lint collects. The mind does that. A single word,
a single thought, a single thing, as Plato taught. We cover our
concepts, like fish, with clouds of net. Cops and bobbies wear
blue. We catch them and connect. Imagined origins reduce the
sounds of clash and contradiction, as when one cries out blue
murder in the street. There's the blue for baby boy, the blue of
blue sky laws, blue for jeans, blue for hogs. The coal fish, a salmon, the glut-herring, a kind of trout, are said to have blue-backs
and are named so in Yorkshire, Maryland, Virginia, Maine. From
earliest times it's been the badge of servitude: among the Gauls,
to humiliate harlots in houses of correction, as the color of a
tradesman's apron, for liveries and uniforms of all kinds, the
varlet's costume.

Blue: bright, with certain affinities for *bael* (fire, pyre), with
certain affinities for bald (*ballede*), with certain affinities for bold.
Odd. Well, a bald brant is a blue goose. And these slippery blue-
green sources ease, like sleeves of grease, each separate use into a

[7]

single—we think—fair and squarely ordered thought machine. Never mind degrees, deep differences, contrasting sizes. The same blue sock fits every leg. Never mind the noses of those Nova Scotian potatoes, blue noses are the consequence of sexual freeze, or they are noses buried far too long in bawdy books, or rubbed too often harshly up and down on wool-blue thighs. Not alone is love the desire and pursuit of the whole. It is one of the passions of the mind. Furthermore, if among a perfect mélange of meanings there is one which has a more immediate appeal, as among the contents of a pocket one item is a peppermint, it will assume a center like the sun and require all others take their docile turn to go around.

This thought is itself a center. I shall not return to it.

Blue postures, attitudes, blue thoughts, blue gestures . . . is it the form or content that turns blue when these are? . . . blue words and pictures: a young girl posed before the door of her family's trailer, embarrassed breasts and frightened triangle, vacant stare . . . I wonder what her father sold the snapshots for? I remember best the weed which grew between the steps. But they say that sexuality can be dangerously Dionysian. Nowhere do we need order more than at any orgy. What is form, in any case, but a bumbershoot held up against the absence of all cloud? Stringy hair, head out of plumb, smile like a scratch across her face . . . my friends brought her image with them from their camping trip, and I remember best the weed which grew between the steps. My sensations were as amateur as her photo. A red apple among oranges. Very beautiful. O God.

Remember how the desperate Molloy proceeds:

I took advantage of being at the seaside to lay in a store of sucking stones. They were pebbles but I call them stones. . . . I distrutibed them equally between my four pockets, and sucked them turn and turn about. This raised a problem which I first solved in the following way. I had say sixteen stones, four in each of my four pockets these being the two pockets of my trousers and the two pockets of my greatcoat. Taking a stone from the right pocket of my greatcoat, and putting it in my mouth, I replaced it in the right pocket of my greatcoat by a stone from the right pocket of my trousers, which I replaced by a stone from the left pocket of my trousers, which I replaced by a stone from the left pocket of my greatcoat, which I replaced by the stone which was in my mouth, as soon as I had finished sucking it. Thus there were still four stones in each of my four pockets, but not quite the same stones. . . . But this solution did not satisfy me fully. For it did not escape me that, by an extraordinary hazard, the four stones circulating thus might always be the same four. In which case, far from sucking the sixteen stones turn and turn about, I was really only sucking four, always the same, turn and turn about.

Beckett is a very blue man, and this is a very blue passage. Several brilliant pages are devoted to the problem. The penultimate solution requires that fifteen stones be kept in one pocket at a time, and moved together—all the stones, that is, which are not being sucked. There is, however, an unwelcome side effect: that of having the body weighted down, on one side, with stones.

. . . I felt the weight of the stones dragging me now to one side, now to the other. So it was something more than a principle I abandoned, when I abandoned the equal distribution, it was a bodily need. But to suck the stones in the way I have described, not haphazard, but with method, was also I think a bodily need. Here then were two incompatible bodily needs, at loggerheads. Such things happen. But deep down I didn't give a tinker's curse about being off my balance, dragged to the right hand or the left, backwards and forwards. And deep down it was all the same to me whether I sucked a different stone each time or always the same stone, until the end of time. For they all tasted exactly the same.

De Sade in a harem of quints could not have faced the issue of love's little nourishments more squarely, or that of the faceless fuck, or equal treatment (stones, wives, Jews, portions of anatomy, don't forget, turn and turn about), and how could one better describe our need for some security in this damn disagreeable/dull dark difficult/disorderly life? And then the resolution, when it comes—is it not a triumph of both will and reason?

> And the solution to which I rallied in the end was to throw away all the stones but one, which I kept now in one pocket, now in another, and which of course I soon lost, or threw away, or gave away, or swallowed.

As we shall see, and be ashamed because we aren't ashamed to say it, like that unpocketed peppermint which has, from fingering, become unwrapped, we always plate our sexual subjects first. It is the original reason why we read . . . the only reason why we write.

It is therefore appropriate that *blow* and *blue* should be—at our earliest convenience—utterly confused.

So I shall, keeping one in each of my four pockets while one is in my mouth, describe five common methods by which sex gains an entrance into literature . . . as through French doors and jimmied windows thieves break in upon our dreams to rape our women, steal our power tools, and vandalize our dreams. The commonest, of course, is the most brazen: the direct depiction of sexual material—thoughts, acts, wishes; the second involves the use of sexual words of various sorts, and I shall pour one of each vile kind into the appropriate porches of your ears, for pronouncing and praising print to the ear is what the decently encouraged eye does happily. The third can be considered, in a sense, the very heart of indirection, and thus the essence of the artist's art—displacement: the passage of the mind with all its blue elastic ditty bags and airline luggage from steamy sexual scenes and sweaty bodies to bedrooms with their bedsteads, nightstands, waterglasses, manuals of instruction, thence to sheets and pillowcases, hence to dents in these, and creases, stains and other cries of passion which have left their prints, and finally to the painted chalkwhite oriental face of amorously handled air and mountains, lewdly entered lakes. The fourth I shall simply refer to now as the skyblue eye (somewhere, it seems to me, there should be a brief pinch of suspense), and the fifth, well, it's really what I'm running into all my inks about, so I had better mention it: the use of language like a lover . . . not the language of love, but the love of language, not matter, but meaning, not what the tongue touches, but what it forms, not lips and nipples, but nouns and verbs.

*   *   *

So *blue*, the word and the condition, the color and the act, contrive to contain one another, as if the bottle of the genii were its belly, the lamp's breath the smoke of the wraith. There is that lead-like look. There is the lead itself, and all those bluey hunters, thieves, those pigeon flyers who relieve roofs of the metal, and steal the pipes too. There's the blue pill that is the bullet's end, the nose, the plum, the blue whistler, and there are all the bluish hues of death.

Is it the sight of death, the thought of dying? What sinks us to a deeper melancholy: sexual incompleteness or its spastic conclusion? What seems to line our life with satin? what brings the rouge to both our cheeks? Loneliness, emptiness, worthlessness,

[11]

grief . . . each is an absence in us. We have no pain, but we have lost all pleasure, and the lip that meets our lip is always one half of our own. Our state is exactly the name of precisely nothing, and our memories, with polite long faces, come to view us and to say to one another that we never looked better; that we seem at last at peace; that our passing was—well—sad—still—doubtless for the best (all this in a whisper lest the dead should hear). Disappointment, constant loss, despair . . . a taste, a soft quality in the air, a color, a flutter: permanent in their passage. We were not up to it. We missed it. We could not retain it. It will never be back. Joy-breaking gloom continues to hammer. So it's true: Being without Being is blue.

Just as blue pigment spread on canvas may help a painter accurately represent nature or give to his work the aforesaid melancholy cast, enhance a pivotal pink patch, or signify the qualities of heavenly love, so our blue colors come in several shades and explanations. Both Christ and the Virgin wear mantles of blue because as the clouds depart the Truth appears. Many things are labeled blue, thought blue, made blue, merely because there's a spot of the color here and there somewhere on them like the bluecap salmon with its dotted head; or things are called blue carelessly because they are violet or purple or gray or even vaguely red, and that's close enough for the harassed eye, the way the brownish halo which surrounds the flame of a miner's safety lamp to warn of firedamp is said to be a bluecap too. Or they are misnamed for deeper reasons: in the ninth century, when the Scandinavians raided Africa and Spain, they carried off samples of the blue men who lived there all the way to Ireland, hence nigger-blue is applied to an especially resinous darkness sometimes by those who are no longer Vikings. And Partridge reports the expression: *the sky as blue as a razor*. Find an eye as blue as indecency itself, an indecency as blue as the smoke of battle, or a battle as blue as the loss of blood. We might remain with such wonders: as blue as . . . as blue as . . . for good and forever.

Anyway, sixth (since the first week had as many working days), I shall describe and distinguish three functions for blue words, modes of production, a Marxist might describe them, and I shall argue that they are equally fundamental. Finally, I shall try to list the major motives, from reader's, work's, and writer's point of view, for introducing blue material in the first place. As blueblaw, blue-blazer, and bluebush. By my private count, you may not be surprised to learn, that makes sixteen separate thoughts I hope to wind my Quink-stained mouth around—turn, of course, and turn about.

II

LET US begin with a brief account of what happened when pirates overtook the whoreship *Cyprian.*

. . . the scene on deck was too arresting for divided attention: the pirates dragged out their victims in ones and twos, a-swoon or awake, at pistol-point or by main strength. He saw girls assaulted on the decks, on the stairways, at the railings, everywhere, in every conceivable manner. None was spared, and the prettier prizes were clawed at by two and three at a time. Boabdil appeared with one over each shoulder, kicking and scratching him in vain: as he presented one to Captain Pound on the quarter-deck, the other wriggled free and tried to escape her monstrous fate by scrambling up the mizzen ratlines. The Moor allowed her a fair head start and then climbed slowly in pursuit, calling to her in voluptuous Arabic at every step. Fifty feet up, where any pitch of the hull is materially amplified by the height, the girl's nerve failed: she thrust bare arms and legs through the squares of the rigging and hung for dear life while Boabdil, once he had come up from behind, ravished her unmercifully. Down on the shallop the sailmaker clapped his hands and chortled; Ebenezer, heartsick, turned away.

Barth is satisfied to say that the girl was ravished unmercifully, but so little is this whole scene tinged with blue that a lively newspaper might carry the account. Rape is on the rise, we read, nearly every day. Now Ebenezer Cooke's servant, Bertrand, an unreliable rogue, is a little distance behind him 'watching with undisguised avidity.' If he had written the passage we would have had a lengthy description of the great Moor's member. Our camera would zoom toward the netted wench until it passed, with him, into her womb. Nor should we find poor Bertram's interest odd, since most of us share it, and, like Gullivers in Brobdingnag, inflate the objects of our greed, deify the origins of every itch, enlarge our lusts, as a coin in the palm of a miser becomes the whole orb of the earth. The deck of the *Cyprian*, however, is not in the world. It needs no hull beneath it, then, no ocean even. It has been wisely noted, in this regard, that we are quite obliged to eat, but there are some perfectly splendid books that never mention the matter.

A crowd of considerations gathers. Here I can pay heed only to a few. It will be observed that Barth, who is a master of the narrative art, modulates the size of his events very carefully, and monitors their pace. It's true that he singles out the girl in the rigging for slightly extended treatment, but this extension is discreet, and even then there is a reason for it: she may be the heroine, Joan Toast.

An author is responsible for everything that appears in his books. If he claims that reality requires his depiction of the sexual, in addition to having a misguided aesthetic, he is a liar, since we shall surely see how few of his precious passages are devoted to chewing cabbage, hand-washing, sneezing, sitting on the stool, or, if you prefer, filling out forms, washing floors, cheering teams.

Furthermore, the sexual, in most works, disrupts the form;

there is an almost immediate dishevelment, the proportion of events is lost; sentences like *After the battle of Waterloo, I tied my shoe,* appear; a sudden, absurd and otherwise inexplicable magnification occurs, with the shattering of previous wholes into countless parts and endless steps; articles of underclothing crawl away like injured worms and things which were formerly perceived and named as nouns cook down into their adjectives. What a page before was a woman is suddenly a breast, and then a nipple, then a little ring of risen flesh, a pacifier, water bottle, rubber cushion. Without plan or purpose we slide from substance to sensation, fact to feeling, all *out* becomes *in*, and we hear only exclamations of suspicious satisfaction: the ums, the ohs, the ahs.

Unless we continue to drain through the cunt till we reach metaphor, as Henry Miller often does:

A dark, subterranean labyrinth fitted up with divans and cosy corners and rubber teeth and syringas and soft nestles and eiderdown and mulberry leaves. I used to nose in like the solitary worm and bury myself in a little cranny where it was absolutely silent, and so soft and restful that I lay like a dolphin on the oyster banks. A slight twitch and I'd be in the Pullman reading a newspaper or else up an impasse where there were mossy round cobblestones and little wicker gates which opened and shut automatically. Sometimes it was like riding the shoot-the-shoots, a steep plunge and then a spray of tingling sea-crabs, the bulrushes swaying feverishly and the gills of tiny fishes lapping against me like harmonica stops.

It's true that Miller occasionally forgets himself. Still, he should be forgiven what we all want: forgetting within the fuck. Love is a nervous habit. Haven't many said so? Snacking. Smoking. Talking. Joking. Alike as light bulbs. Drinking. Drugging. Frigging. Fucking. Writing. Forgetting. Nerves. Nerves, nerves,

nerves. Our author does not, in fact, get sufficiently inside his line, forget enough to be forgiven. He talks too much, compulsively, his memory is made of suspiciously precise lies, the overlarge anecdotal detail—yowl, stance, and quim size, garlic and onion, vestibule or stairway—like one of those guides at the Vatican.

∗   ∗   ∗

The common deer in its winter coat is said by hunters to be in the blue. To be in the blue is to be isolated and alone. To be sent to the blue room is to be sent to solitary, a chamber of confinement devoted to the third degree. It's to be beaten by police, or, if you are a metal, heated until the more refrangible rays predominate and the ore is stained like those razor blades the sky is sometimes said to be *as blue as*, for example, when you're suddenly adrift on a piece of cake or in a conversation feel a wind from outer space chill your teeth like a cube of ice. Ah, but what is form but a bum wipe anyhow? Let us move our minds as we must, for form was once only the schoolyard of a life, the simple boundary of a being who, pulsating like an artery, drew a dark line like Matisse drew always around its own pale breath. Blue oak. Blue poplar. Blue palm. There are no blue bugs of note, although there are blue carpenter bees, blue disk longhorn beetles, blue-winged wasteland grasshoppers, one kind of butterfly, bottle-fly, the bird, and not a single wasp or spider. The muff, the fur, the forest, and the grot.

So it always is as we approach the source of our desires. As Rilke observed, love requires a progressive shortening of the senses: I can see you for miles; I can hear you for blocks; I can smell you, maybe, for a few feet, but I can only touch on contact,

[18]

taste as I devour. And as we blend, sight, the sovereign sense and concept's chief content, blurs. 'The lover,' Rilke wrote, 'is in such splendid danger just because he must depend upon the co-ordination of his senses, for he knows that they must meet in that unique and risky centre, in which, renouncing all extension, they come together and have no permanence.'

A flashlight held against the skin might just as well be off. Art, like light, needs distance, and anyone who attempts to render sexual experience directly must face the fact that the writhings which comprise it are ludicrous without their subjective content, that the intensity of that content quickly outruns its apparent cause, that the full experience becomes finally inarticulate, and that there is no major art that works close in. Not an enterprise for amateurs. Even the best are betrayed.

Caspar Goodwood suddenly takes Isabel Archer in his arms: 'His kiss was like white lightning, a flash that spread and spread again, and stayed . . .' and Henry James, quite unconsciously, goes on to say that 'it was extraordinarily as if, while she took it, she felt each thing in his hard manhood that had least pleased her, each aggressive fact of his face, his figure, his presence, justified of its intense identity and made one with this act of possession.' But he never made this mistake again.

The blue lucy is a healing plant. Blue john is skim milk. Blue backs are Confederate bills. Blue bellies are Yankee boys. Mercurial ointment, used for the destruction of parasites, is called blue butter, although that greenish-blue fungus we've all seen cover bread is named blue-mold instead.

So Barth wisely remarks that the lady was ravished unmercifully and turns his hero sadly away. But the deck of the *Cyprian* is not in this world. Would we be content here, where we are, napkin at neck, to stare distantly at our beef, to receive reports that we had eaten without the pleasures of the chewing? No— only close-ups will content us here. We approach, indeed, until it's entered us. The difference between 'the beef' and 'the blue' may seem at the same time too wide and too narrow to be of significance. Although, in many ways, these appetites are quite alike, there is no comparable literary mode dedicated to the seared and steaming flank; the mark of every tooth is nowhere with joy recorded; the floods of saliva, the growls which empty from the throat, the delight of every bite and swallow, the slice of the knife, its grate on the plate beneath, the hot . . . the glands groan as I describe it . . . the spicy hot sauce in which the sausage swims . . . there's no Homer for them; there's no Henry Miller either, or Akbar del Piombo; there's only James Beard and Julia Child, masters of the shopping list.

As writers we don't hesitate to interrupt murders, stand time on its tail, put back to front, and otherwise arrange events in our chosen aesthetic order, but how many instances of such *coitus interruptus* are there in the books which speak to us so frankly of the life we never frankly lead? how often does insertion come before erection, weak knees anticipate the kiss?

I should like to suggest that at least on the face of it a stroke by stroke story of a copulation is exactly as absurd as a chew by chew account of the consumption of a chicken's wing.

✳   ✳   ✳

The worship of the word must be pagan and polytheistic. It cannot endure one god. The Scots use blue brilliantly, for instance, and have their own term, *blae*, for gray blue, lead blue, and livid. The hedge-chanter is better known to them as the blue hafit, and if we pursue their names for the lumpsucker or sea owl, a fish of uncouth appearance, we come upon *bluepaidle*, or the even more common *cockpaidle*. The dictionary is as disturbing as the world, full of teasing parallels and misleading coincidence. The same fish is called a paddlecock on account of the tubercular skin which envelopes its dorsal ridge and which resembles the comb of that barnyard lord.

Suppose the name of any maiden's private part were known to her alone. Suppose the name of Ellen's pout were Rosalie. Then that name, if we came into possession of it, would argue an intimacy for us no parent or lover could overlook, as though we had been privy to the mole on her mount of Venus. From the first 'In the beginning . . . ' words have been thought to have magical properties. They can, we are assured by authorities, persuade, snare, frighten, bless. They can stimulate, damn, anger, kill, caress. If signs are not the same as the things they designate, they are at least an essential segment, so that to speak the word, Rosalie, is to be halfway to Ellen's occupation. Look how the blood rises in her bottle-skinny neck. What was naïve in the magician was the belief that things have names at all, but equally naïve are the learned and reasonable who reject any connection beyond the simply functional between *blue* and blue, Ellen's beard and Rosalie. Words are properties of thoughts, and thoughts cannot be thought without them. We are truly *in the blue*, and if we try to think blue without thinking *blue*, we are forced into euphemism: Ellen's pretty promenade, we say, Ellen's merry whiskered friend, the South Pole Santa Claus, and so forth.

Which brings us to *Fanny Hill*, a dirty book without a dirty word; nor is the work as successfully suggestive as its title. There are plenty of explicitly sexual scenes, but 'amorous engine' is as blunt as Cleland can bring himself to be. He had a deep sense for the blush in blue language. As Christian Enzenberger has recently observed:

> Its [language's] reaction to smut is inevitably one of impotence if not downright hostility. It resists, begins to stammer, if dirty words have to be pronounced it does so, but sulkily, dutifully as it were, in the most unfeeling way, which is to say by means of onomatopoeia; in short, language becomes as embarrassed as the speaker himself and prefers to take refuge in indirect speech. (*Smut: an Anatomy of Dirt*)

Lars Porsena or the Future of Swearing and Improper Language, a slight light blue book, was written in the twenties. There its author, Robert Graves, repeats Samuel Butler's definition of Nice People as 'people with dirty minds' in order to point out that his book was written for Nice People like that, and partly to apologize for its discretions.

> Observe with what delicacy I have avoided and still avoid writing the words x——— and y———, and dance round a great many others of equally wide popular distribution. I have yielded to the society in which I move, which is an obscene society: that is, it acquiesces emotionally in the validity of the taboo, while intellectually objecting to it. I have let a learned counsel go through these pages with a blue pencil and strike through paragraph after paragraph of perfectly clean writing.

These scrupulosities are no longer necessary. I do not practice them. Yet I cannot honestly say I see any noteworthy improvement in our life, thought, or writing, now that 'fuck' can be heard and seen in public, because its appearance is as unmeant and hypocritical as its former absence was. We fear to seem a prude. We fear also the loss of revenues. So we green pencil in the penis, then yellow it out for prick. Cock is okay but only schoolboys have dicks. Thus civilization advances by humps and licks.

Of course every soldier-sport-and-buddy book believes that you can't kill either animals or people without swearing at something first. Since one honors the animals one is about to murder, you must swear at your beaters. There are no girls in foxholes, as everyone knows, so there's no occasion for sex (we should smile in our amorous wisdom at this remark); there is much manliness, however, which consists of saying 'shit' with every breath you haven't used up spitting. Each rifle is erect. It would be hard to imagine a work in which there were all sorts of words for dogs, cats, and cows, their natures and parts (as in the expression, 'by doggies'), without a single animal appearing in it (certainly not a dog, a cat, or a cow), but this is normal in the literature of strong (that is to say, embarrassed) speech. Strength of this kind, of course, is the visible side of weakness, and requires a special use for language which I should like to set aside for mention later.

The following verses from World War I, which Graves quotes, illustrate nicely the imaginative meanness of tough talk.

THE AUSTRALIAN POEM

A sunburnt bloody stockman stood,
And in a dismal, bloody mood
Apostrophized his bloody cuddy:
'This bloody moke's no bloody good,

He doesn't earn his bloody food,
Bloody! Bloody! Bloody!'

He leapt upon his bloody horse
And galloped off, of bloody course.
The road was wet and bloody muddy:
It led him to the bloody creek;
The bloody horse was bloody weak,
'Bloody! Bloody! Bloody!'

He said, 'This bloody steed must swim,
The same for me as bloody him!'
The creek was deep and bloody floody.
So ere they reached the bloody bank
The bloody steed beneath him sank—
The stockman's face a bloody study
Ejaculating Bloody! bloody! bloody!

There are a number of difficulties with dirty words, the first of which is that there aren't nearly enough of them; the second is that the people who use them are normally numskulls and prudes; the third is that in general they're not at all sexy, and the main reason for this is that no one loves them enough.

Contrary to those romantic myths which glorify the speech of mountain men and working people, Irish elves and Phoenician sailors, the words which in our language are worst off are the ones which the worst-off use. Poverty and isolation produce impoverished and isolated minds, small vocabularies, a real but fickle passion for slang, most of which is like the stuff which Woolworths sells for ashtrays, words swung at random, wildly, as though one were clubbing rats, or words misused in an honest but hopeless attempt to make do, like attacking tins with toothpicks; there is a dominance of cliché and verbal stereotype, an abundance of expletives and stammer words: you know, man, like wow! neat, fabulous, far-out, sensaysh. I am firmly of the opinion that people who can't speak have nothing to say. It's one more thing we do to the poor, the deprived: cut out their tongues . . . allow them a language as lousy as their lives.

Thin in content, few in number, consantly abused: what chance do the unspeakables have? Change is resisted fiercely, additions are denied. I have introduced 'squeer,' 'crott,' 'kotswinkling,' and 'papdapper,' with no success. Sometimes obvious substitutes, like 'socksucker,' catch on, but not for long. What we need, of course, is a language which will allow us to distinguish the normal or routine fuck from the glorious, the rare, or the lousy one—a fack from a fick, a fick from a fock—but we have more names for parts of horses than we have for kinds of kisses, and our earthy words are all . . . well . . . 'dirty.' It says something dirty about us, no doubt, because in a society which had a mind for the body and other similarly vital things, there would be a word for coming down, or going up, words for nibbles on the bias, earlobe loving, and every variety of tongue track. After all, how many kinds of birds do we distinguish?

We have a name for the Second Coming but none for a second coming. In fact our entire vocabulary for states of consciousness is critically impoverished.

The forbidden words may be forbidden, but we sneak them in. First we pretend to be using another word which happens to resemble the forbidden one exactly, as in this exchange between

[25]

Romeo and Mercutio. Romeo begins:

> *Is love a tender thing? it is too rough,*
> *Too rude, too boistrous, and it pricks like thorn . . .*

To which Mercutio replies:

> *If love be rough with you, be rough with love;*
> *Prick love for pricking, and you beat love down . . .*

Prick, cock, screw, balls, bust, bang, suck, lick . . . the list is endless, and endlessly uninteresting.

The raw rude word may appear submerged, as when an angry Hamlet asks Ophelia if he may lie in her lap, and she says:

> *No, my lord.*
> *I mean, my head upon your lap.*
> *Aye, my lord.*
> *Do you think I meant country matters?*

. . . a line in which 'cunt' is concealed by a tree.

> *I think nothing, my lord.*
> *That's a fair thought to lie between maids' legs.*
> *What is, my lord?*
> *Nothing.*

There is the love inside of glove, the ass in brass, the dung in dungeon, and even the pee in perspective. It is necessary to rub the little-boy smirk off these words before they can be used with any success, and introducing them in these angular ways sometimes helps. Although rarely.

The fact is: they aren't loved enough. Almost every English poet writes of love and fornication, enjoys describing women as if they were fields awaiting subdivision. Does not our Dr. Donne, himself, cry out: Oh, my America, my new-found-land? Indeed.

[26]

But he keeps the language clean. When it comes to sexual directness and plain speech, Burns probably surpasses, but even he has
the advantage of a dialect extraordinarily rich in sweet blue
words like gamahuche* and

> Then gie the lass her fairin', lad,
>   O gie the lass her fairin',
> An' she'll gie you a hairy thing,
>   An' of it be na sparin';
> But lay her o'er amang the creels,
>   An' bar the door wi' baith your heels,
> The mair she gets, the mair she squeals,
>   An' hey for houghmagandie.

. . . which may account for the fact that I could never take Ma-
hatma Gandhi very seriously.

Walt Whitman, who was indeed daring in his day, was rarely
convincing. In truth, America's great maker of lists was usually
sappy:

> This is the female form.
> A divine nimbus exhales from it from head to foot,
> It attracts with fierce undeniable attraction,
> I am drawn by its breath as if I were no more than a helpless
>   vapor, all falls aside but myself and it,
> Books, art, religion, time, the visible and solid earth, and
>   what was expected of heaven or fear'd of hell,
>   are now consumed,
> Mad filaments, ungovernable shoots play out of it, the response
>   likewise ungovernable,

---

*It has the feel, the taste, of the Scots, even though it is French.

Hair, bosom, hips, bend of legs, negligent falling hands all
*   diffused, mine too diffused,*
Ebb stung by the flow and flow stung by the ebb, love-flesh
*   swelling and deliciously aching,*
Limitless limpid jets of love hot and enormous, quivering jelly
*   of love, white-blow and delirious juice,*
Bridegroom night of love working surely and softly into the
*   prostrate dawn,*
Undulating into the willing and yielding day,
Lost in the cleave of the clasping and sweet-flesh'd day.

Poets who would never meter their stick or brag of their balls;
who would never vulgarly vaunt of their lady's vaginal grip or
be publicly proud of her corpulent tits, succumb to the menace
of measurement. Rossetti, while he kisses, counts.

Her arms lie open, throbbing with their throng
Of confluent pulses, bare and fair and strong:
And her deep-freighted lips expect me now
Amid the clustering hair that shrines her brow
Five kisses broad, her neck ten kisses long . . .

Lately, Yeats approached the problem, and Pound had occasional success, the most notable, I suppose, this passage from
Canto XXXIX:

Desolate is the roof where the cat sat,
Desolate is the iron rail that he walked
And the corner post whence he greeted the sunrise.
In hill path: 'thkk, thgk'
*   of the loom*
'Thgk, thkk' and the sharp sound of a song

> under olives
> When I lay in the ingle of Circe
> I heard a song of that kind.
> Fat panther lay by me
> Girls talked there of fucking, beasts talked there
> of eating,
> All heavy with sleep, fucked girls and fat leopards,
> Lions loggy with Circe's tisane,
> Girls leery with Circe's tisane . . .

Lovely as this is, the rest of his frankness is in Latin and Greek.

No, they are not well-enough loved, and the wise writer watches himself, for with so much hate inside them—in 'bang,' in 'screw,' in 'prick,' in 'piece,' in 'hump'—how can he be sure he has not been infected—by 'slit,' by 'gash'—and his skills, supreme while he's discreet, will not fail him? Not an enterprise for amateurs. Even the best are betrayed. Lawrence is perhaps the saddest example.

✳   ✳   ✳

There's the blue skin of cold, contusion, sickness, fear . . . absent air, morbidity, the venereals, blue pox . . . gloom . . .

There are whole schools of fish, clumps of trees, flocks of birds, bouquets of flowers: blue channel cats, the ash, beech, birch, bluegills, breams, and bass, Andalusian fowl, acaras, angels in decorative tanks, the bluebill, bluecap, and blue billy (a petrel of the southern seas), anemone, bindweed, bur, bell, mullet, salmon, trout, cod, daisy, and a blue leaved and flowered mountain plant called the blue beardtongue because of its conspicuous yellow-bearded sterile stamens.

The mad, as we choose to speak of others who do not share our tastes, provide cases galore of color displacement: they think pink is blue, that brown is blue, that sounds are blue, that overshoes are condoms, and we have only to describe these crazies directly and they will smuggle the subject in all by themselves. Freud thought that a psychosis was a waking dream, and that poets were daydreamers too, but I wonder if the reverse is not as often true, and that madness is a fiction lived in like a rented room. The techniques, in any case, are similar.

Here is Thick, in *The Lime Twig* of John Hawkes, beating Margaret:

'I've beat girls before,' whispering, holding the truncheon in the dark, bracing himself with one fat hand against the wall, 'and I don't leave bruises. . . . And if I happened to be without my weapon . . . the next best thing is a newspaper rolled and soaking wet. But here, get the feel of it, Miss.' He reached down for her and she felt the truncheon nudging against her thigh, gently, like a man's cane in a crowd.

'It ain't so bad,' he whispered.

She was lying face up and hardly trembling, not offering to pull her leg away. The position she was tied in made her think of exercises she had heard were good for the figure. She smelled gun oil— the men who visited the room had guns—and a sour odor inside the mattress. . . . There was a shadow on the wall like a rocking chair; her fingers were going to sleep; she thought that a wet newspaper would be unbearable.

Then something happened to his face. . . .

His arm went up quivering, over his head with the truncheon falling back, and came down hard and solid as a length of cold fat stripped from a pig, and the truncheon beat into her just above the knee; then into the flesh of her mid-thigh; then on her hips; and on the tops of her legs. And each blow quicker and harder than the last, until the strokes went wild and he was aiming randomly at abdomen and loins, the thin fat and the flesh that was deeper, each time letting the rubber lie where it landed then drawing the length of it across stomach or pit of stomach or hip before raising it to the air once more and swinging it down. It made a sound like a dead bird falling to empty field. . . . When he finally stopped for good she was bleeding, but not from any wound she could see.

This passage is impossible to overpraise . . . an example of total control: get the feel of it, Miss . . . a man's cane in a crowd . . . a length of cold fat stripped from a pig . . . a dead bird falling to empty field . . . she thought that a wet newspaper would be unbearable.

When a character will not oblige by using a truncheon as a penis, the author must manage the shift himself. Flaubert directs our eyes to the room in which Emma Bovary commits her adulteries, and has the sense, so often absent in his admirers, to be content with that.

The warm room, with its discreet carpet, its grey ornaments, and its calm light, seemed made for the intimacies of passion. The curtain-rods, ending in arrows, their brass pegs, and the great balls of the fire-dogs shone suddenly when the sun came in. On the chimney between the candelabra there were two of those pink shells in which one hears the murmur of the sea if one holds them to the ear.

A muff, a glove, a stocking, the glass a lover's lips have touched, the print of a shoe in the snow: how is it that these simple objects can receive our love so well that they increase it? I answer: because they become concepts, lighter than angels, and all the more meaningful because they began as solids, while the body of the beloved, dimpled and lined by the sheeted bed, bucks, sweats, freezes, alters under us, escapes our authority and powers, lacks every dimension, in that final moment, but the sexual, yet will not remain in the world it's been sent to, and is shortly complaining of an ache. The man with his fetish, like a baby with its blanket, *has* security—not the simple physical condition (with locks on the doors who is safe?) but the Idea itself. Those pink shells, the curtain-rods ending in arrows, the great balls of the fire-dogs: how absurd they would be in reality, how meaningless, how lacking in system, all higher connection. It's not the word made flesh we want in writing, in poetry and fiction, but the flesh made word.

> 'Léa. Give me your pearls. Do you hear me, Léa? Give me your necklace.'

And shortly this remarkable book has begun, like a head between breasts, to surround us with Colette's unsurpassed sensuality.

> There was no response from the enormous bed of wrought-iron and copper which shone in the shadow like a coat of mail.
> 'Why don't you give me your necklace . . . ?'
> As the clasp snapped, the laces on the bed were roused and two naked arms, magnificent, with thin wrists, lifted two lovely lazy hands.
> 'Let it alone, Chéri . . .'

The images are chosen as the pearls were: the bed, the light, the sheets, the pearls, the laces which rouse . . .

> In front of the pink curtains barred by the sun he danced, black as a dainty devil on a grill. But as he drew near the bed he became white again in silk pyjamas above doe-skin mules.

There is anger in the eyebrows knotted above his nose, a mutinous mouth, the deep bed like a warm pond . . .

> He opened his pyjamas on a chest that was lusterless, hard and curved like a shield: and the same pink high-light played on his

teeth, on the whites of his black eyes and on the pearls of the necklace.

Not a single indecency defines this indecent scene.

Colette has the cat's gaze. Unhurried contemplation is her forte. Hunger cannot give us such precision.

> Meanwhile the shadows lengthened on the beach; the blackness deepened. The iron black boot became a pool of deep blue. The rocks lost their hardness. The water that stood round the old boat was dark as if mussels had been steeped in it. The foam had turned livid and left here and there a white gleam of pearl on the misty sand.

The nouns in this passage are all nailed too firmly to their *thes*; otherwise Virginia Woolf's construction here is sensuous in the same way as Colette's: observant, thoughtful, loving, calm.

$$* \quad * \quad *$$

Pink and white and the blackbird black of Chéri's glistening hair are the colors Colette has chosen for Léa's and his encounter —pink, black, and white, and the copper decoration of the bed— but blue is our talisman, the center of our thought. Yet what blue? which? the blue that settles in the throat before the cough? that rounds from our mouth like a ring of smoke as we announce *A noir, E blanc, I rouge, U vert, O bleu?* Not the blue of place names like Blue Island or Blue Bay. The Blue Hens Chickens. Not the blue of all the fish or flowers which have obtained it, the trees, the minerals, or the birds, not even the blue of blue pigeon, the sounding lead, which is none of these. Perhaps it is the blue of reality itself:

> Blue is the specific color of orgone energy within and without the organism. Classical physics tries to explain the blueness of the sky by the scat-

tering of the blue and of the spectral color series in the gaseous atmosphere. However, it is a fact that blue is the color seen in all functions which are related to the cosmic or atmospheric or organismic orgone energy:

Protoplasm of any kind, in every cell or bacterium is blue. It is generally mistaken as 'refraction' of light which is wrong, since the same cell under the same conditions of light loses its blueness when it dies.

Thunder clouds are deeply blue, due to high orgone charges contained in the suspended masses of water.

A completely darkened room, if lined with iron sheet metal (the so-called 'Orgone Room'), is not black, i.e., free of any light, but bluish or bluish-gray. Orgone energy luminates spontaneously; it is 'luminescent.'

Water in deep lakes and in the ocean is blue.

The color of luminating, decaying wood is blue; so are the luminating tail ends of glowworms, St. Elmo's fire, and the aurora borealis.

The lumination in *evacuated tubes charged with orgone energy* is blue.

(Wilhelm Reich: *The Orgone Energy Accumulator—Its Scientific and Medical Use*)

The word itself has another color. It's not a word with any resonance, although the *e* was once pronounced. There is only the bump now between *b* and *l*, the relief at the end, the whew. It hasn't the sly turn which crimson takes halfway through, yellow's deceptive jelly, or the rolled-down sound in brown. It hasn't violet's rapid sexual shudder, or like a rough road the irregularity of ultramarine, the low puddle in mauve like a pancake covered with cream, the disapproving purse to pink, the assertive brevity of red, the whine of green. What did Rimbaud know about the vowels we cannot also find outside the lines in which the poet takes an angry piss at Heaven? The blue perhaps of the aster or the iris or the air a fist has bruised?

[34]

'The lights burn blue; it is now dead midnight,' Shakespeare wrote. 'Pinch the maids as blue as bilberry . . . ' 'Her breasts, like ivory globes circled with blue/A pair of maiden worlds unconquered . . . ' And so to the worst: 'Her two blue windows' (here he means the eyelids of reviving Venus) 'faintly she up-heaveth.' Blue Eagle. Blue crab. Blue crane. Blue pill. Blue Cross.

But our sexual schemes scarcely need the encouragement of a common word, the blues with which I began, for instance: blue pencils, blue noses, blue movies . . . Throw down any pair of terms like dice; speak of arrogant bananas; command someone, as Gertrude Stein once did, to 'argue the earnest cake,' and the mind will do more than mix them in its ear. It will endeavor a context in which the command is normal, even trite. Our grammars give us rules for doing that, but sometimes these are no more than suggestions. Our interests do the same. Just as a man who is sick with suspicion may suppose that even the billboards are about him, any text can be regarded as a metaphorical description of some subject hidden in the reader's head. In that blue light which lust (or orgone energy) is said to shine on everything, we begin to see what an arrogant banana might be. Adolescent boys may live for weeks within a single sexual giggle, and when political life feels the thumb, then any innocent surface (poor Turgenev's *A Sportsman's Notebook*) can conceal a call to arms. Suppressed material contaminates the free like fecal water. *Ernani* or *The Marriage of Figaro* become revolutionary.

Out of aching puberty, I remember very well a burlesque skit to which I was a breathless, puzzled witness much the way I once watched, through a slit, slogans scribbled on a washroom wall by a large rotund little man who held his hand to his heart as though he were warming it, and rolled down his lower lip. Press-

[35]

ed Pants is telling Baggy of his wonderful trip to Venice, and how a beautiful woman invited him to take a ride in her gondola (a word which both pronounced *gone-dough-la*).

You're kidding. You actually got in her gondola.
She invited me, I told you. She practically insisted.
Listen . . . hey . . . tell me: what was her gondola like?
Oh, you know, they're all pretty much the same—long and narrow, a bit flat-bottomed, with a tall ornamental stem.
Boy. Oh boy. I can't believe it. And you got in?
Spent the whole afternoon.
In her gondola?
Sure. Saw all the sights.
Ah, come on . . . naw . . . not all afternoon.
Sure. At first we went fast but later we just took it easy and lay there kinda lazy. She was well built, soft and cushiony inside. We had tea and cake, too, and a good long discussion about art.
While you was still in her gondola?
Certainly. She didn't rock much. And there was a fiddler—huge guy —who played lively little tunes the whole time. And sang a few romantic songs, and pointed out the points of interest.
Wow. I'll bet. But he wasn't in her gondola too?
Sure he was—where would he be?
Ah, come on now . . . Naw . . . Naw . . . He was in there while you was? at the same time?
Naturally. To fiddle. Yeah. It was a big gondola. There was plenty of room.

For the prude, or his political equivalent, there are dangerous suggestions in the most carefully processed air; there are lewd insinuations, Commie connivance; any word may yawn indecently, or worse, a gondola may engulf us; yet unless we are privately obsessed, something in the text or context must sound the proper political or sexual alert (Condition Blue is the second stage of any warning system), and if the soberness of some occasions is

[36]

sufficiently impressive, even loud alarms may clang quite vainly, as you often have to tug the reader's sleeve before he'll hear a bladder making Joyce's *Chamber Music*, or, while fingering one of the *Tender Buttons* Miss Stein has designed, feel somewhere a little tingle.

Mental sets are essential to every art, and various cheap jokes can be made of them. Here is one such which Sir John Suckling, who was capable of better, should never have composed:

> *There is a thing which in the light*
> *Is seldom us'd; but in the night*
> *It serves the female maiden crew,*
> *The ladies and the good-wives too;*
> *They used to take it in their hand,*
> *And then it will uprightly stand;*
> *And to a hole they it apply,*
> *Where by its goodwill it would die;*
> *It spends, goes out, and still within*
> *It leaves its moisture thick and thin.*

There have been many riddles of this kind, although, led to expect that the answer to the question, 'What is it?' will be 'penis,' and being told with a triumphant smirk that it is 'candle' instead, we may with some annoyance put that dubious object back into the poem to function as a dildo rather than a light.

The purest tale can still be blue, given a big blue eye, as that crafty old pornographer, Samuel Richardson, demonstrated more than once; for instance, when he wrote *Pamela*, the edifying history of a prick tease—a book bluer than any movie.

* * *

Aching puberty indeed. The awkward figure in that snapshot I referred to earlier was the first completely naked woman I had ever seen, and her very awkwardness, the cheapness of the camera, the amateurishness of print, pose, and light, the commonplace reality of the trailer, made her bewildered breasts and puffy pubic hair yearningly real too, as if the photograph were a doorway or a window opening toward a nudity so ordinary it might have been anyone's—mine—yours—yes, in just that way it was a window, became a door, and although I felt sorry for the girl and even shared her humiliation, I stared—ashamed of my own heat—her helplessness as exciting as her sex—I stared—I lapped her up, left the picture-paper clean as a cat's saucer; because finally, when one day I looked, she was no longer there, not even the weed caused any commotion. The window had pulled its own shade. So like a sultan I soon gave her away since she was once again only a fifty-cent image, an eyeful at the boy-pull and occasion for a furtive jerk.

Yet what had I seen when I stared? She was so girlish and so naked, so simply there, that a description of her, had I attempted it, would have failed for want of attention. Too real to be pornographic, I saw not the forbidden image but the forbidden object of that image, the great mystery itself, the subject of a thousand dreams, a hundred thousand stories. I saw what all my organs seemed to stir for . . . and I took fright. Were her breasts like ivory globes circled with blue, then? were they a pair of maiden worlds unconquered? Of course not, but I would have wanted to think so. Fuddle-eyed innocence can only say, Gee Whiz. And the knowing writer—whose carnal knowledge begins with Gee Whiz and ends at Ho Hum without apparently stopping at any

[38]

station in between—hunts among his comparisons like Wilde through his wardrobe for something he may have handy of a suitably similiar color, size, softness, and value.

Perhaps mounds of ice cream topped by a cherry? slopes of virginal snow, alabaster idols, golden apples, hills and hummocks, berries? ah, of course, a plump pair of pillows.

The singer of the Song of Solomon declares that the breasts of his beloved are two graceful young roes, that they are clusters of grapes, that they are towers; but I am not prepared to believe this crook-carrying poet, whose mind is exclusively on money, food, drink, and the increase of his herds.

> 1 Behold, thou art fair, my love; behold thou art fair; thou hast doves' eyes within thy locks: thy hair is as a flock of goats, that appear from mount Gilead.
> 2 Thy teeth are like a flock of sheep that are even shorn, which came up from the washing; whereof every one bear twins, and none is barren among them.
> 3 Thy lips are like a thread of scarlet, and thy speech is comely: thy temples are like a piece of pomegranate within thy locks.
> 4 Thy neck is like the tower of David builded for an armoury, whereon there hang a thousand bucklers, all shields of mighty men.
> 5 Thy two breasts are like two young roes that are twins, which feed among the lilies.

These comparisons are always unfairly one-sided and often reveal, as in the singer above, an unpleasant preference for perfume, property, and plunder. One may decide that the nipple most nearly resembles a newly ripened raspberry (never, be it noted, the plonk of water on a pond at the commencement of a drizzle, a simple bladder nozzle built on the suction principle, gum bubble, mole, or birth wart, bumpy metal button, or the painful red eruption of a swelling), but does one care to see his breakfast fruit as a sweetened milky bowl of snipped nips? no.

There's something of the thimble to them (not enough), and they are frequently described as rosy or said to possess the color of young shoots, but why take the trouble when the trouble taken is so evident and audible and yields such frigid results? Perhaps they are like the lightly chewed ends of large pencil erasers. Yes. When brown, they are another pair of eyes. Or is it the eyes which promise me those rich wide aureoles? I have seen nipples so pulled on and flattened by nursing, they hung there like two tiny tongues.

D'Annunzio may write that 'long trailing vapours slid through the cypresses of the Monte Maria like waving locks through a comb of bronze,' and though the comparison is highly decorative, it is not absurd to imagine on the obverse of the metal a maiden's blond tresses, as she prepares her hair for a night of love, passing through the tines of her comb of bronze like trailing vapours through a row of cypresses. But may I comfortably think of those sheep as wandering teeth?

There's no tit for tat in this poetry, which is, after all, the sort of erotic verse preferred by those who once loved to listen (and if they could, would still, sweet dears) to Madame Melba, freshly risen from her death as Mimi and now surrounded by bouquets, while accompanying herself on a baby grand wheeled opportunely from the wings to the center of an emptied stage, warble 'Home Sweet Home' and 'The Last Rose of Summer' in the intervals of silence between applauding palms.

Oh! ah! ai! alack and alas! *ahimè!* but what is love? how best speak of the beauty of women? account for the soul's deep swoons without confusing them with the greedy swoops of a gull

[40]

after herring? explain the blue of serge or chicory, or ordinary sky, the iris and the pansy blue of melancholy, the still intenser blue of the imagination?

It is Orlando's problem too, and Orlando finds that every subject he (and he will not suffer his sex change until the eighteenth century) wishes to pursue so embroiled, cluttered, and betangled with every other that it appears impossible for him to say a single, simple, clear, true thing.

> . . . he tried saying the grass is green and the sky is blue and so to propitiate the austere spirit of poetry whom still, though at a great distance, he could not help reverencing. 'The sky is blue,' he said, 'the grass is green.' Looking up, he saw that, on the contrary, the sky is like the veils which a thousand Madonnas have let fall from their hair; and the grass fleets and darkens like a flight of girls fleeing the embraces of hairy satyrs from enchanted woods. 'Upon my word,' he said (for he had fallen into the bad habit of speaking aloud), 'I don't see that one's more true than another. Both are utterly false.' And he despaired of being able to solve the problem of what poetry is and what truth is and fell into a deep dejection.

Conrad also rather bitterly complained, regarding the precision of his elected language, that writing in English was like throwing mud at a wall. But blueness fuddles every tongue like wine.

Pierre Louys, whose credentials are impeccable, being both French and pagan, at least achieves originality:

> Thy breasts are two vast flowers, reversed upon thy chest, whose cut stems give out a milky sap. Thy softened belly swoons beneath the hand.

However, I fear that Dr. Johnson would find his effort too metaphysical.

We appear to be reduced to apostrophe: the elegant Gee Whiz. Certainly nothing else will do for fellatio, which has never had its poet. Even our aforementioned D'Annunzio, by training perfectly equipt, cannot do much more than moan ornately.

> O sinuous, moist and burning mouth, where my desire is intensified when I am sunk in deep oblivion, and which relentlessly sucks my life. O great head of hair strewn over my knees during the sweet act. O cold hand which spreads a shiver and feels me shivering.

Yet in the moment that our situation seems to have become impossible (as bereft of hope as Virginia Woolf's Orlando has imagined it to be), *deus ex machina*: we recollect the honest masters of our tongue, and in them, on occasion, we find the problem solved, the tribute paid, the vision pure, the writing done. In Ben Jonson, for instance:

> *Have you seene but a bright Lillie grow,*
> *Before rude hands have touch'd it?*
> *Ha' you mark'd but the fall o' the Snow*
> *Before the soyle hath smutch'd it?*
> *Ha' you felt the wooll of Bever?*
> *Or Swans Downe ever?*
> *Or have smelt o' the bud o' the Brier?*
> *Or the Nard in the fire?*
> *Or have tasted the bag of the Bee?*
> *O so white! O so soft! O so sweet is she!*

Initially I wrote of displacement as if it went from thing to thing—phallus to flower:

> *Full gently now she takes him by the hand,*
> *A lily prison'd in a gaol of snow,*
> *Or ivory in an alabaster band;*
> *So white a friend engirts so white a foe . . .*

but I have been dropping hints all along like heavy shoes that the

[42]

ultimate and essential displacement is to the word, and that the true sexuality in literature—sex as a positive aesthetic quality—lies not in any scene and subject, nor in the mere appearance of a vulgar word, not in the thick smear of a blue spot, but in the consequences on the page of love well made—made to the medium which is the writer's own, for he—for she—has only these little shapes and sounds to work with, the same saliva surrounds them all, every word is equally a squiggle or a noise, an abstract designation (the class of cocks, for instance, or the sub-class of father-defilers), and a crowd of meanings as randomly connected by time and use as a child connects his tinkertoys. On this basis, not a single thing will distinguish 'fuck' from 'fraise du bois'; 'blue' and 'triangle' are equally abstract; and what counts is not what lascivious sights your loins can tie to your thoughts like Lucky is to Pozzo, but love lavished on speech of any kind, regardless of content and intention.

It is always necessary to deprive the subject of its natural strength just as Samson was, and blinded too, before recovering that power and replacing it within the words. Popeye is about to rape Temple Drake with a corn-cob (in a corn-crib, too, if you can bear the additional symbolism):

> . . . Popeye drew his hand from his coat pocket.
> To Temple, sitting in the cottonseed-hulls and the corn-cobs, the sound was no louder than the striking of a match: a short, minor sound shutting down upon the scene, the instant, with a profound finality, completely isolating it, and she sat there, her legs straight before her, her hands limp and palm-up on her lap, looking at Popeye's tight back and the ridges of his coat across the shoulders as he leaned out the door, the pistol behind him, against his flank, wisping thinly along his leg.

[43]

He turned and looked at her. He waggled the pistol slightly and put it back in his coat, then he walked toward her. Moving, he made no sound at all; the released door yawned and clapped against the jamb, but it made no sound either; it was as though sound and silence had become inverted. She could hear silence in a thick rustling as he moved toward her through it, thrusting it aside, and she began to say Something is going to happen to me. She was saying it to the old man with the yellow clots for eyes. 'Something is happening to me!' she screamed at him, sitting in his chair in the sunlight, his hands crossed on the top of the stick. 'I told you it was!'

Forty pages pass before Temple Drake begins to bleed.

It wasn't nice of Thick to beat Margaret either, and I really don't know if he did it beautifully or not, but Hawkes's account is beautiful. Stones will never nourish us however patiently or hard we suck them. What fills us then, in such a passage?

It is Beckett's wonderful rhythms, the way he weighs his words, the authority he gives to each, their measured pace, the silences he puts between them, as loving looks extend their objects into the surrounding space; it is the contrapuntal form, the reduced means, the simple clear directness of his obscurities, and the depth inside of every sentence, the graceful hurdle of every chosen obstacle, everywhere the lack of waste.

Compare the masturbation scene in *Ulysses* with any one of those in *Portnoy*, then tell me where their authors are: in the scene as any dreamer, night or day, might be, or in the language where the artist always is and ought to be.

If any of us were as well taken care of as the sentences of Henry James, we'd never long for another, never wander away: where else would we receive such constant attention, our thoughts anticipated, our feelings understood? Who else would robe us so richly, take us to the best places, or guard our virtue as his own and defend our character in every situation? If we were his sentences, we'd sing ourselves though we were dying and about to be extinguished, since the silence which would follow our passing would not be like the pause left behind by a noisy train. It would be a memorial, well-remarked, grave, just as the Master has assured us death itself is: the distinguished thing.

III

WHEN, with an expression so ill-bred as to be fatherless, I enjoin a small offensive fellow to 'fuck a duck,' I don't mean he should. Nothing of the sort is in my mind. In a way I've used the words, yet I've quite ignored their content, and in that sense I've not employed them at all, they've only appeared. I haven't even exercised the form. The command was not a command. 'Go fly a kite' only looks like 'shut the door.' At first glance it seems enough that the words themselves be shocking or offensive—that they dent the fender of convention at least a little —but there is always more to anything than that.

For example, when rice is thrown at a newly wedded pair, we understand the gesture to have a meaning and an object. Sand thrown at the best man misses its mark. Yet the rice, too, is being misused—neither milled, planted, nor boiled. Of course, rice signifies fertility for us. It resembles (indeed is) a seed. It is small and easily handled. It is light and lands lightly on its targets. It is plentiful and easily come by. And it is cheap. In short, rice is like *three cheers*, *good luck*, and *God speed*. Rice is like language. Similarly, when we swear we say we let off steam by throwing our words at someone or at something. 'Fuck you,' I mutter to the backside of the traffic cop, though I am innocent of any such intention.

Crude as it is, the case allows us to separate what is meant from what is said, and what is said from what is implied, and what is implied from what is revealed. Cursing dares convention and defies the gods, yet, as conventional itself as the forms it flouts, cursing does not dare defy the conditions of wholesome clarity, and 'fuck a duck' is admirable in that regard. Nor did I labor to invent the phrase. No one invents them. 'Jesus Christ on a raft,' an expostulation of my youth, did not catch on. I may choose to throw rice at newlyweds, but I do not—cannot—create the gesture. 'May shit fall upon you from a biplane' will hardly earn a medal for the imagination; nevertheless it is clearly something someone composed, and therefore not a curse at all, but a joke (as 'fuck a duck' is). At great cost, comedians have such curses composed for them. They often concern camels.

Although the expression *says* 'hunt up a duck and fuck it,' the command quite routinely *means* 'go away; pursue some activity suitable to your talents, something disgusting and ineffectual like fucking a duck.' Nonetheless, of all the fish and fowl, all the plants, animals, images, and other elements of the earth which provide some sort of aperture, it was the *uck* in 'fuck' that selected 'duck.' I might have said 'fuck a fox'; however, the modulation of *uck* into *ox* is too sophisticated for swearing, and a fox has, in every way, the nobler entry. 'Fuck a trucker' is equally sound (though it tails off doggily), but the command calls for courage and so scarcely carries the same disdain. In these days when letters to the editor may contain instructions on how to masturbate with a vacuum cleaner, cucumber, or cantaloupe, the directive, 'fuck a fruit,' has become facetiously indeterminate. I happen to like 'fuck a lock,' nevertheless this phrase proves my point. One may admire its subtle comparison of 'pick' with 'prick,' or the happy resonance of 'lot' and 'lock,' or that humorous reference to the chastity belt, but successful swearing can afford to be baroquely outrageous only if it also remains as straightforwardly open and sharp and quick as a slap.

In 'go to hell' and 'fuck you,' the words have been glued together by thoughtless use and mindless custom. We do not speak them the way we speak ordinary sentences. They are not said, but recited, like *ave marias*; so if I say 'damn you' and really mean you to be damned by a vengeful god at my behest, I have said 'damn you' the way I daily say 'let's eat,' and that is a way no one says 'damn you' any more, because curse-blue sentences are made of welded parts like the bumpers of automobiles, while with this revitalized 'damn you,' I have tried to make the phrase the way I once made ferris wheels and towers out of tinkertoy by following instructions.

Swearing consists of a series of cultural quotations, and although others may have said 'let's eat' before me, and although I may have said 'let's eat' many times already myself, I am not reciting or quoting, repetition is no part of my intention, I am hungry again, that's all; while if I say, to the lady lying under me, 'hurry up, please, it's time,' I am quoting, and my fucking may be quoting, too, if it endeavors to recover another copulation and a previous joy by magical adherence to the past.

Crude as it is, then, the case allows us to separate sentences and phrases which are truly created from those which are merely routine; and those which are squeezed out of daily life like the juice of a lime, however customary, from those which are tongued or sung or spelled or recited. The sentences of ordinary speech, of hunger and seduction, gossip and commerce, are sewn from patterns, put together according to blueprints and plans. We have been taught several simple ways to ask for water, grant physical favors, spare a dime. For water, 'water!' does very well, and anything much more complicated, anything original, discriminating, or interior, suggests that our thirst is not any deeper than the bottom of our throat.

'Fuck you,' I mutter to the backside of the traffic cop. Fuckyous are in fact the principal item of macho exchange. Since I do not want to fuck the cop I must want someone else to, and since that ubiquitous 'you' is almost certainly another male (as it is in this instance), I can only desire your sodomization. To be entered as a woman is, to be so demeaned and reduced and degraded: for us gaucho machos, what could be worse? In a business deal, if you find you have been screwed, what should have been *up theirs* is disconcertingly *up you*. These aggressive wishes, expressed so fervently and often and in practiced ignorance of their meaning, reveal the depth of the desire for buggery among our bravos and our braves.

So 'fuckyous' are welded and spelled rather than stitched or freely created. They say, 'fuck you,' but they mean, 'may you suffer a sex change.' They imply defiance, and reveal a desire for power. Furthermore, in the Freudian sense, they disguise certain sodomous inclinations. Fucked-up situations fuck us up. They make us ineffectual and passive. Since the power cursing requests is never forthcoming, one's actual impotence is hid by a

[50]

small act of verbal defiance. 'Piss on you' is a relatively straight-forward dominance claim. 'Shit on you' serves the same function. All these anal-sex-and-smear swears serve the same function, and are largely interchangeable like turds, for one stool is as good as another in the democracy of the mouth.

Crude as they are, such cases force us to distinguish not only between *use* and *mention*, as logicians normally do, but also between these and what might be called simple *utterance* or outcry. Key chains, drapes, and dishes are used, wagonwheels, tuning forks, whistles, words. What else are they for? Drapes hang heavily from their bars. Chains key. Wheels turn. Pass the butter. Take off your bra. The Blue Ridge Mts. are in Virginia. Or they may instead be mentioned, as I shall this moment mention 'swive,' a term which Barth has beautifully blown his breath upon and thus attempted to revive. I, myself, have had no success with 'grampalingus,' 'meatus foetus,' or 'mulogeny'—a sentence which, if you could not see the quotes around the words you might think meant I'd tried them all and failed. Well, no one listens to what they see.

In babyhood and through moist infancy, the penis is a 'pee-pee.' When worn by boys, it becomes a 'peter' or a 'dick.' Later we refer to the instrument (even our own, and not, alas, unhappily) as a 'whang.' We call it a 'dong.' We say it is a 'dork.' Imagine. Meanwhile, the lovely Irish 'langolee,' or 'wheedledeedle,' my concoction, get no backers. Though 'bluebeard' and 'blue-skin' have once upon a time been used, no one is forgiven. Still, in a world of prick-skinning women, perhaps a twanger is what one needs. These days are drear. However . . . 'fuck,' in 'go fuck a duck,' is neither used nor mentioned; it is merely *uttered*. These

[51]

'fucks' are phatic like the delivery of 'good morning,' the wearing of evening clothes, giving of handshakes, painting of smiles, adding the complimentary close.

Most of the time we are content to cry out 'fuck!' as if pinched, but the function of our wall words in slightly more elaborate curses, such as:

> may your cock continue life as a Canadian,
> or
> may the houseflies winter over in your womb,
> or
> may you be inhaled by your own asshole,

is more complex. Although each expression is merely uttered (curses without a curse, they contain only archery and cleverness like a purse full of chocolates and needles), every element has an internal use, so that we can say that single words can be used within mention or mentioned within use, mentioned in an utterance or uttered in a mention, uttered in an utterance, mentioned in a mention, and so on like a fugue. This cleverness in one sense mitigates the shock by calling attention to the quirks and capabilities of the mind that shapes the mouth that makes them, just as those obnoxious little jokes which leap like startled frogs into the center of every conversation do, or those pointless puns some damply nervous souls are obsessively driven to compose. In any case, their *being* lies in their *occurrence*.

It is not alone words about which these distinctions can be profitably made, and I hope the difference will help interpret many of my earlier remarks. If I shed my clothes to make love or take a shower, I am using my nakedness; if I wear a daring gown, I may be mentioning it; but the bared behinds on the modern stage aren't mentioning themselves, nor are they ever used. They are merely uttered. I know situations where the devil has appeared with no more function than a shout. This is often the role of the star who doesn't do anything but twinkle. In the *Cantos*, Pound only mentions his Chinese words, he rarely really uses them. Although the sexual descriptions of the pornographer are frankly employed to produce erection, and the sex in Kinsey or Kraft-Ebbing is mentioned for the sake of study, the sex in *Oh, Calcutta!* is simply sworn.

The blue list with which I began was celebrational. I did not use the phrase 'blue devil' but I was delighted to mention it: blue line, blue note, blue plate. If I were uttering these words (as I am presently trying to formulate the distinction), I would not particularly care what they meant, I would only care what people thought of their appearance in my speech: would they think them friendly, or not; appropriate, or not; predictable, or not? And consequently I would only care what people thought of *me* for using them: blue nevus, blue vinny, bluetongue, blue tangle, blue star, blue bells. Noises or notes: what do I care? What is their public pay-off for me?

Unfortunately these three—utterance, mention, and use—as well as the other distinctions I've dragged across the page, are overly crude, and have names which mislead beside. Their cuts are like cracks between buttocks, and philosophy should be ashamed to contain them in such an untrained, yappy, and pissy condition. There is, first of all, a more fundamental bifurcation, overriding every other, namely between those blues whose continued existence is as obnoxious as a pile of sanitary napkins, the blues we expect to dispose of after use (or utterance or mention), those we've set fire to, or eaten, or blown our noses in, those blues, in short, which appear to disappear, and are otherwise linguistic waste:

gee, look at the little blue butterfly,
or
give us a B, give us an L, give us a BLU,
or
how am I? glad you asked, yes, well, yesterday
I was kinda gray, but today I'm downright blue,
or
buster, baby, you bastard, you blew it.

No one wants that sullied air and spoiled paper about. There are acts which we are glad are gone and gone without a trace, too: gaucheries, spit-ups and spraying sneezes, broken promises, prematurities of all kinds, arguments and chores, the one-night stands with fortunately not a single fuzzy Polaroid to bluemail them or piece of tape to tangle. There are thoughts, postures, attitudes of the same sort, consciousness itself, some say, who regard it as no more than the belching of the body . . . and who wants a collection of throat-farts fastened though floating around their source like a tree full of soft blue Italian plums?

Then there are the blues we'd love to have loom large and linger long around us like deep sofas, accommodating women, and rich friends: the blues in dictionaries, grammars, spelling books; the blues in all the manuals that lay out figures, facts, and their relations, so definitively we continue to consult them . . .

the Eastern Tailed Blue,
Dwarf Blue,
Pigmy Blue,
Common Blue,

or Spring Azure, whose larvae secrete what the ants call 'honeydew,'
the Western Tailed Blue,
Square-spotted Blue,
Acmon Blue,
Orange-bordered or Melissa Blue,
which has two broods,
Reakirt's Blue,
which feeds on mesquite,
the Silvery Blue,
Sonora Blue,
Saepiolus Blue,
. Marine Blue,

whose worms chew upon locoweed and the blossoms of the wisteria, or the blues of the great poems . . .

ix

And the color, the overcast blue
Of the air, in which the blue guitar

Is a form, described but difficult,
And I am merely a shadow hunched

Above the arrowy, still strings,
The maker of a thing yet to be made;

The color like a thought that grows
Out of a mood, the tragic robe

Of the actor, half his gesture, half
His speech, the dress of his meaning, silk

Sodden with his melancholy words,
The weather of his stage, himself.

(Wallace Stevens: 'The Man with the Blue Guitar')

or the emblematic blues, the color in which Joyce bound *Ulysses*, its title like a chain of white islands, petals shaken on a Greek sea, he thought, and the heraldic blues, the celebrational and symbolic . . .

> Gargantua's colors were white and blue. . . . By these colors, his father wished to signify that the lad was a heavenly joy to him. White expresses joy, pleasure, delight and rejoicing; blue denotes things celestial.
> I realize quite well that, as you read these words, you are laughing at the old toper, for you believe this symbolic use of colors to be crude and extravagant. White, you say, stands for faith, and blue for strength. But without getting excited, losing your temper, flying into a rage or working yourself into a tongue-parched passion—the weather is dangerous—tell me one thing! . . . What moves, impels or induces you to believe what you do? Who told you that white means faith, and blue strength?
> 'A shoddy book,' you reply, 'sold by peddlers in remote mountain hamlets and by weatherbeaten hawkers God knows where. Its title? *In Praise of Colors.*'

or the blues we rebreathe, always for the same reason: because the word in each case finds its place within a system so supremely organized it cannot be improved upon—what we would not replace and cannot change. Of how many racy tales or hairy photos can that be said?

So sentences are copied, constucted, or created; they are uttered, mentioned, or used; each says, means, implies, reveals, connects; each titillates, invites, conceals, suggests; and each is eventually either consumed or conserved; nevertheless, the lines

[56]

in Stevens or the sentences of Joyce and James, pressed by one another into being as though the words before and the words after were those reverent hands both Rilke and Rodin have celebrated, clay calling to clay like mating birds, concept responding to concept the way passionate flesh congests, every note a nipple on the breast, at once a triumphant pinnacle and perfect conclusion, like pelted water, I think I said, yet at the same time only another anonymous cell, and selfless in its service to the shaping skin as lost forgotten matter is in all walls; these lines, these sentences, are not quite uttered, not quite mentioned, peculiarly employed, strangely listed, oddly used, as though a shadow were the leaves, limbs, trunk of a new tree, and the shade itself were thrust like a dark torch into the grassy air in the same slow and forceful way as its own roots, entering the earth, roughen the darkness there till all its freshly shattered facets shine against themselves as teeth do in the clenched jaw; for Rabelais was wrong, blue is the color of the mind in borrow of the body; it is the color consciousness becomes when caressed; it is the dark inside of sentences, sentences which follow their own turnings inward out of sight like the whorls of a shell, and which we follow warily, as Alice after that rabbit, nervous and white, till suddenly—there! climbing down clauses and passing through 'a^{n}d' as it opens—there—there—we're here!... in time for tea and tantrums; such are the sentences we should like to love—the ones which love us and themselves as well—incestuous sentences —sentences which make an imaginary speaker speak the imagination loudly to the reading eye; that have a kind of orality transmogrified: not the tongue touching the genital tip, but the idea of the tongue, the thought of the tongue, word-wet to part-wet,

[57]

public mouth to private, seed to speech, and speech . . . ah! after exclamations, groans, with order gone, disorder on the way, we subside through sentences like these, the risk of senselessness like this, to float like leaves on the restful surface of that world of words to come, and there, in peace, patiently to dream of the sensuous, imagined, and mindful Sublime.

✳   ✳   ✳

Half-breeds belong to the blue squadron. Sometimes they are called 'blue skins,' as Protestants once were. *Blue Boy* is the popular title of a painting by Gainsborough, the name of a prize hog in *State Fair*, and the abscess from a venereal disease. Under the vilifying gaze of fluorescent light, the heads of pimples turn blue, as do the rings around the eyes, and the lips grow cold. Although the form, 'blueness,' signifies the quality of being blue in any sense, it usually refers only to indecency: *les horreurs, les bêtises, les gueulées.* Will it profit us to wonder why? Jackson Pollock painted *Blue Poles*, the name of any magnet's southern dart. Earlier he'd covered a canvas he labeled *The Blue Unconscious*. Here the color is sparingly used. A group of Germans got itself called the *Blaue Reiter*, and Piero della Francesca did indeed make the Virgin's mantle blue in his *Annunciation* . . . in his *Nativity*, too. Nor did the Lorenzettis neglect her, Giotto neither, though he colored his pit-of-hell devils blue as a soul dismantled. Contending that art is a product of pain, Picasso passed through such a period, painting *The Blue Room, Woman in Blue,* and many others: stem-like bodies on which long faces gather like solidifying smoke.

'For our blues,' Hoogstraten says, 'we have English, German, and Haarlem ashes, smalts, blue lakes, indigo, and the invaluable ultramarine.' It is of course the sky. It is the sky's pale deep endlessness, sometimes so intense at noon the brightness flakes like a fresco. Then at dusk, it is the way the color sinks among us, not like dew but settling dust or poisonous exhaust from all the life burned up while we were busy being other than ourselves. For our blues we have the azures and ceruleans, lapis lazulis, the light and dusty, the powder blues, the deeps: royal, sapphire, navy, and marine; there are the pavonian or peacock blues, the reddish blues: damson, madder and cadet, hyacinth, periwinkle, wine, wisteria and mulberry; there are the sloe blues, a bit purpled or violescent, and then the green blues, too: robin's egg and eggshell blue, beryl, cobalt, glaucous blue, jouvence, turquoise, aquamarine. A nice light blue can be prepared from silver, and when burned, Prussian blue furnishes a very fine and durable brown. For our blues we have those named for nations, cities, regions: French blue, which is an artificial ultramarine, Italian, Prussian, Swiss and Brunswick blues, Chinese blue, a pigment which has a peculiar reddish-bronze cast when in lump-form and dry, in contrast to China blue which is a simple soluble dye; we have Indian blue, an indigo, Hungarian, a cobalt, the blues of Parma and Saxony, Paris, Berlin, and Dresden, those of Bremen and Antwerp, the ancient blues of Armenia and Alexandria, the latter made of copper and lime and sometimes called Egyptian, the blue of the Nile, the blue of the blue sand potters use. Are there so many states of mind and shades of feeling? In a dress riddled with polka dots, Colette, arthritic and frizzy in her final photographs, sits with the profile of Cocteau, *le fanal bleu,* her papers and her pain. And for our blues we have those named for

[59]

persons, processes, and earths: Hortense, Croupier, Blackley blue and Chemic, Imperial or spirit-blue, Raymond or Napoleon blue, Night blue or Victoria, Leitch's blue, Schweinfurth's or Reboulleau's blue, Monthier's blue, which uses ammonia, Elberfeld, Eschel, Gentiana blue, Gold blue, Guernsey, Guimet, Humboldt and the coal-tar colors, Aniline, Alkali, Anthracene blue, Alizarin blue, paste blue, vat blue, fast blue, the fluorescent resorcinol blues, milori, vitriol, blue verditer, slate and steel blue, all the grays, gun-metal, asbestos, and then the bluish shades of verdigris appearing subtly in the same way that our attitudes slowly acetify our bodies. Fra Angelico, that sweet man, did not ignore the Virgin either, though her mantle, alas, is never blue, but sometimes lavender or even green. 'Green' is another name, though now forgotten, long unused, for things obscene.

Long unused. Still, the disappearance from literature of words and subjects (or their appearance there) simply because writers and readers have strong feelings about them is never an aesthetically promising cause. And the principal difficulty with using sexual material in literature is that the motives of all concerned are usually corrupt.

Because of the values we place on sexuality in life, because of the terrible taboos which surround it, the endless lies, the forlorn wishes, the sad fantasies we wind around it like gauze about a wound (whether these things are due to the way we are brought up, or are the result of something graver—an unalterable quality in our nature), everyone's likeliest area of psychological weakness is somewhere in the sexual. Writers, whose work is actually an analogue anyway, are still more susceptible to the blue disease, so that even those whose mastery of their medium is otherwise incontestible will—with a serious air—plait flowers in their hero's pubic hair and stumble over a little fornication like a toddler climbing stairs. Any author's wisdom here consists of the correct assessment of his own weaknesses and the discovery of technical ways to circumvent them. Not an enterprise for amateurs. Colette used the blue paper she wrote on to shade her writing light . . . to shine bluely through the curtains at pedestrians crossing the Palais-Royal a notice of her presence day and night.

But we are perfectly familiar with these things.

＊　　＊　　＊

> *Those dressed in blue*
> *Have lovers true;*
> *In green and white,*
> *Forsaken quite.*

> *Touch blue,*
> *Your wish will come true.*

> *If you love me, love me true,*
> *Send me a ribbon, and let it be blue;*
> *If you hate me, let it be seen,*
> *Send me a ribbon, a ribbon of green.*

It is intriguing to wonder whether the difficulties children have with color, the quickness with which they pick up forms and functions and learn the names for bye-bye, truck, and auntie, yet at a late age (even five), without a qualm, call any color by the name of any other, aren't found again in the history of our words, for oysters could not be oozier than these early designations. Blue is blue or green or yellow: what the hell. Or so it seems. Colors flood our space so fully that there isn't any. They allow us to discriminate among otherwise identical things (gold and green racing cars, football teams, jelly beans, red- brown- blond- and black-haired girls); however, our eye is always at the edge, establishing boundaries, making claims, so that colors principally enable us to discern shapes and define relations, and it certainly appears that patterns and paths—first, last, and in between—are what we want and what we remember: useful contraptions, useful controls, and useful connections.

Yet the pig in the pigment is missing. Well, what do we need with all that fat? Our world could be gray as the daily paper and we'd not miss much in the way of shapes and sizes. An occasional bluebird might be overlooked fleeing extinction through a meadow—so what. As much an afterhue as afterthought, colors came to the movies as they came to the comics, and there they remain—surreal in their overlays—like bad printing. Hoopla is hoopla however it's hollered. Tinting that weed green or its trailer silver would not have improved my naked girl's gray and white image. No. Who cares for color in a world of pure trans-missions?

Children collect nouns, bugs, bottlecaps, seashells, verbs: what's that? what's it doing now? who's this? and with the greed which rushes through them like like rain down gulleys, they im-mediately grasp the prepositions of belonging and the pronouns of possession. But how often do they ask how cold it is, what color, how loud, rare, warm, responsive, kind, how soft, how wet, how noxious, loving, indiscreet, how sour?

Measures, not immersions, concerned our sciences almost from the beginning, and we were scarcely out of the gate before Democritus was declaring fiercely that 'color exists by convention, sweet by convention, bitter by convention; in truth nothing exists but the atoms and the void.' Although Anaxagoras had already claimed that we see nothing but light reflected in the pupil of the eye, the real organ of perception, all along, was Mind. It was the soul that saw for Plato, too, yet color was a dissembling cosmetic, the tinted marble and the gilded thigh, perfume for the iris, spice for spoiled meat, and when the mind put a public face on, as Protagoras might, or Gorgias did, in pursuit of persuasion, it painted itself like an old whore for the light, and with one finger gooey from the color pot circled its sockets with the pale cream and gray-blue grit of the shaven pubis, smearing on each cheek a paste which matched the several pallors of debauchery, though these undertoning blues and violets were startled sometimes by spots of cantharidian red, or else with the whole hand it spread a melancholy which gently purpled the spent body like a bruise.

For Democritus, shape was the principal cause of color, especially the shape of what might be considered the reflecting or emitting surface: white atoms were smooth, black jagged (shadow-casting, Theophrastus suggests); though his account is hardly consistent since the atoms of red are compared to those of flame and simply said to be larger, while the ones which produce green are made, like the statues of Henry Moore, of the solid and the void itself—thing and no thing—which, according to his own teaching, is the way the whole of reality is put together and not just the greenish part. Moreover, Democritus omitted blue from the list of his primary colors at the cost of our admiration.

On the other hand, Epicurus claimed that the positions and arrangements of the atoms were as important as their isolated shape, and that, in effect, color's cause was molecular, an opinion more correct than he could ever have imagined, since hue is not the simple effect of a stimulus, it is the actual perception of a whole series or set of relations.

In any case, as Galen observed, very early the philosophers kicked quality out of science. Aristotle insisted that qualities were accidents and could not be a part of essence. Lucretius faithfully followed the lead of Epicurus. Galileo was equally concerned to reserve physics for mathematics, and, as we know, Descartes delivered, as a Frenchman should, the *coup de grâce*.

The campaign against quality was a campaign against consciousness, because that's where quality was thrown like trash in a can. Although Descartes' public purpose was to certify faith, his successful secret purpose was to clean up thought for the surgeries of science. For the most part, then, qualities were removed from the external world and given over to that same soul which was once said merely to perceive them, as though the telescope with its lenses had swallowed the stars. It is important to notice, however, that Plato's complaint about color was not that it was illusory whereas the physical world which it concealed was real. No, for him the dancer was as deceitful as her veils. The intercourse of eye and object, which involves the voluptuous intertwining of two rays (these were his own blue metaphors), engenders twins: the eye is filled with seeing (an activity), while simultaneously the object seen becomes luminous with color (a condition). Eye and sky together are then blue and its apprehension. Goethe—great pagan that he was—sounds the same note:

The eye owes its very existence to light. From inert animal ancillary organs light evokes an organ which shall become light; and so the

[64]

eye learns to give light for light, emitting an internal ray to encounter that from without.

Plato's brilliant and beautiful suggestion avoids the insoluble
projection problem. Of course, in philosophy, you settle one bill
only by neglecting another, a strategy which must eventually be
seen to fail since all of them fall due at the same time. Nevertheless, Plato was never guilty of such unempirical foolishness as the
rag-taggle of doctrines which crowded along afterward required.
Once spread across the spaceless night and total nowhere of the
soul, how shall the stars be got back through the skull and eye
and scope into the sky again? No one has ever come close to saving
and explaining the objective appearance of perception, not even
Schopenhauer, whose suggestion was at least a try: namely that
perception was a process in which a felt effect, in the moment of
its existence, was nevertheless always experienced as if it were
occurring in the space of its cause, and that understanding was
simply the ability to experience any such effect farther and farther back along the chain of its conditions or its grounds.

Ordinary inferences are not altered by the time it takes to
make them. Here, however, immediacy is essential. In short,
'seeing' the blue of the gentian, the storm in the clouds, or deer
in their tracks, involved the same principles and was basically the
same process. Genius, then, was the ability to 'see' a long way—
swiftly. Unfortunately, the implication is that if I were stupid
enough—retarded might be the right word—I would see no
farther than the inside of my eye. This seems unlikely, and, although the dunce sits in the corner he's been sent to, the corner
does not close that narrowly upon him, or his conical paper
crown slide that darkly to his nose.

Aristotle had no more doubt than Plato did that things were loud, sour, blue, or rough, but he had difficulty in understanding how we saw and felt and heard these qualities. Moreover, he wished to avoid Plato's dismissal of the sensible world as a ground for knowledge. Consequently, he was driven to make a number of extraordinary suggestions. Perception, he said, is the power of receiving 'the sensible forms of things without their matter.' Here we tremble on the brink of something without actually toppling in, because Aristotle's sensible forms, transmitted to us through an intervening medium called 'the transparent,' are tinted images, visible species, the verdigris of bronze without the bronze, the shape of the spear, first in the trembling air and then in the eye, given to us as the sharp flowing edge of a set of colors; but like a camera which peels off and spools the visible film of things, what these colors color must be supplied by the sensitive soul itself.

We reach that brink in the moment when Aristotle says:

> ... the sense is affected by what is coloured or flavored or sounding, but it is indifferent what in each case the *substance* is; what alone matters is what *quality* it has, i.e., in what *ratio* its constituents are combined. ...

When a colored surface sets the transparent in motion, it relays to the eye a record of the relation between light and dark which constitutes its hue, and the organ responds by establishing this relationship inside itself. Thus

> ... the actualities of the sensible object and of the sensitive faculty are one actuality in spite of the differences between their modes of being ...

and the mind flies to another essay, this time a contemporary one by Edwin H. Land, in which the results of his experiments on color vision are summarized. It is not the eye's response to a single wavelength, as the spectrum displays them, which causes us to perceive a color, rather

> ... the colors in a natural image are determined by the relative balance of long and short wavelengths over the entire scene ... ('Experiments in Color Vision')

so that within the frequencies which make up spectral yellow, for instance, the whole range of colors can be experienced. Within spectral blue, already short or cool, the cool side will be seen as blue, the long or warm side as red. Clearly, color is the experience of a ratio.

As I should like to spell the theory now, the musician, for example, counting on the auditory laws, creates a structure he knows the mind will materialize in sounds of a certain kind. The musical score represents the music's form in ink and paper. The disc represents it in wiggles and rounds. The performance troubles the air with the same structures. And our mind *hears*. But the qualities we taste in wine, touch and feel along the thigh while loving, hear as singing, sniff from the steaming pot, or observe articulate the surface of a painting, are, in fact, relations. Furthermore, the sense of passion or of power, of depth and vibrancy, feeling and vision, we take away from any work is the result of the intermingling, balance, play, and antagonism between these: it is the arrangement of blues, not any blue itself, which lets us see the mood it formulates, whether pensive melancholy or thoughtless delight, so that one to whom aesthetic experience comes easily will *see*, as Schopenhauer suggested, sadness in things as readily as smoky violet or moist verdigris.

[67]

Nevertheless, what we saw, Aristotle had to say, was *not quite* the color as it was embedded in its bronze. It was instead a color generalized, the species bluegreenbrownishness, expressed, to be sure, in an individuating medium of its own, yet like the particular twangs of native speech, easily replaced with Oxford's universal intonations by any listener fastidious enough to care. Furthermore, these qualities, although slightly general in their character, were neither essential nor universal enough to figure importantly in knowledge. The shapes of things, wrapped like cigars in their shades, were informative sometimes, but perception mainly permitted us to establish the behavior patterns of plants, animals, and things, and having sequences, discover causes, hence general laws and universal schemes. In short: without color we could not perceive, nor, I suspect, remember, but the production of these qualities is never part of the basic activity of Being, and therefore an account of them is never a significant part of natural science.

Will the Bishop do better by blue? After all, he appeals to common sense and to the experience of ordinary men. Yet

> It is an opinion *strangely* prevailing amongst men, that houses, mountains, rivers, and in a word all sensible objects have an existence natural or real, distinct from their being perceived by the understanding.

No one betrays perception more promptly than the empiricist. First he appeals to common sense, which he flouts; then to experience, which he misrepresents. How far must we search to find the reason for this strangely prevailing opinion? As it happens, the cover of my copy of Berkeley's *New Theory of Vision* is blue, and when I shelve it so the sides slide between Bergson and

[68]

Bradley, do they cease to be blue or bluish or even any color? Do I ever feel the likelihood of that, or wonder at the possibility?

No doubt Berkeley was right to remind us that all our statements about the qualities of things are reducible to the general prediction that if we carry out certain operations properly, we will have certain perceptions; but it does not follow from this that *to be* is *to be perceived*; rather we must be content to argue only that to be *known* to be is to be perceived, for there is no other way to 'know' perceptible qualities except by perceiving them.

Am I then wrong to believe that my copy of Berkeley remains blue though it rests in my briefcase throughout the night? Am I deceived if I think that the blue belongs to the book, not to me, though the book has my name on its flyleaf and lives on my shelves quite contentedly? Am I mistaken to maintain that this blue is a public property, as much as a park, for all to see, though my leather case and library are as private before the law as the penis behind my pants? Have I been fooled if I feel that this blue, though only a color, will suffer fading and staining, a circuit of changes like everything else on its way to oblivion? Suppose I shelve my book backward so that its raw ends stick out. How do I know that the binding has not fled with the blue I can't see, like Peter Pan to the land of lost children, and the pages are held between Bradley and Bergson like a rosary between praying palms?

Don't prate to me of divinity, dear Bishop, but of blue, the godlike hue, because it's contrary to experience to assume that anything alters itself without cause; consequently I can feel certain that my Berkeley will remain blue so long as I can be confident that there is no plot afoot to dye, bleach, or rebind it. The Law of Inertia will serve us all more reliably than the allegedly omniscient though in truth often watery gaze of God.

Thomas Reid, a Scot who not only believed in common sense but used it, wrote with some exasperation once that

> Every man feels that perception gives him an invincible belief of the existence of that which he perceives; and that this belief is not the effect of reasoning, but the immediate consequence of perception. When philosophers have wearied themselves and their readers with their speculations upon this subject, they can neither strengthen this belief, nor weaken it; nor can they show how it is produced. It puts the philosopher and the peasant upon a level; and neither of them can give any other reason for believing his senses, than that he finds it impossible for him to do otherwise. (*Essays on the Intellectual Powers of Man*)

Still, every one of these diligent gentlemen may be right . . . and why should we mind if every one of them is right simultaneously? Let all notes sound together and cacophony be king.

There are particular pieces of the world which essentially serve the abstract (dominos, for instance, standing armies, monetary prose), and there are fragments of the mind which nevertheless pretend to be (like men of good will and the data of sense) residents in the realm of things. It is around these coins, twin-headed and treacherous, that the quarrel which concerns us has centered, for there is clearly a similar conflict between the way we customarily experience color and the way we have historically tended to think about it. This unnecessary antagonism is traditional: shall we believe our senses or our reason? And reason is so swift to slander the senses that even Hume did not escape, replacing shadow, mood and music, iris and jay, with a scatter of sense impressions artificial as buttons: each distinct, inert, each intense, each in self-absorbed sufficiency and narrowly circumscribed disorder like a fistful of jelly beans tossed among orphans or an army of ants in frightened retreat.

The blunt truth is that if the sky's not blue, the sea, the serge suit, the chicory, the blue goose; if they're not blue, then, like our ears and nose and tongue and fingers, our eyes have lied, and although on occasion the truth may be beaten from them, they cannot be a standard; they have soiled consciousness too continuously; they cannot be trusted. If, on the other hand, we begin with what we're given, then what about all those advisers who have whispered persuasive nonsense in our ears from the beginning? don't believe what you hear—the violin, the wind— believe me; others feel differently, in other ages, different climes; even yourself—on grayer days, at greater distances, in sickness, out of madness, during dream—distort—from pique, from spite, from wine; remember the shadows which threatened you like a thief? the friend you greeted like a stranger? the lap dog's bite? the lips which claimed to be so sweet? so don't believe the rainbow or the oil, but believe the lines the mind conceives con- nect the spill and bow to you; believe in the weights of spaces and the rush of quantity through the void. Well? what to do? For their treachery, for the buttered sound of their sophistries, shall we confine them to the tower?

Choose.

* * *

We might suppose that connoisseurs and critics of painting, certainly the painters themselves, would be better disposed to blue than the physicists and philosophers—that's a natural thought—and we might expect many of them to think of shape as a qualification of color, or colors as contents whose limits were created simply to contain them, like thick cream curdling in a bowl (because who looks at the basket when it's heaped with berries?)—yes, that's a thought natural enough—but you also might expect writers to love their words (does not Krapp cry out 'spooooool' to the unrecorded walls of his room?), although the truth is that what they usually want is whatever their words represent (the things, not the thoughts, the things, not the sounds, the things, not the snicker and giggle of ink or the rumple of sentences like slept-in pajamas—no, only things, dear things, sweet things . . . and then only those things things designate, the way work means money and money downpays the car and cars confer status and status is power and power converts to cash), just as painters have for centuries carefully colored between the lines, lines which everyone read as the edges of objects, of things, though the color of those things, the mantle of the Virgin, for instance, sometimes gave them a special meaning.

Yes, once blue signified, not sky, but Heaven, against which the figures of the gods burned like suns. Off and on it stood for the great outdoors, the container of all those usefully precious and precarious things; it was the space of spaces, the big Big Sky, and blue would flow into rooms through windows or surround soldiers, tall trees, towns, a flagellated Christ, with Greek, Venetian or Egyptian light as clean and final as a fluttering cape or goodbye shawl. Occasionally it darkened like a pit in which the world was thrown, or now and then it threatened us with the come-hither recessions of its vertiginous deeps, and we were small and incomplete before it as men had been in earlier times before their mountain-dwelling divinities.

Seldom was blue for blue's sake present till Pollock hurled

pigment at his canvas like pies. Rarer still, since such sensitivity in the brush tip is a rarity (in the penis rarer, in the poet rarest of all), color became the breath of bodies, every hue the aching limit of a life, as if it rose up from within the substance it covered the way feeling changes the color of the chameleon, or like those remarkable cephalopods whose configurations alter with their moods, or as, inadequately, our own blood comes and goes like sunshine dreaming among moving clouds.

Consequently, there is not only filmy cover-color like fur and clothing, as Adrian Stokes suggests, or color which leaps from things like sparks from hammered spikes or sifts through the atmosphere like dust or crowds near the eye like a swarm of gnats, in contrast to objects which appear self-lit, but the surfaces of painted figures can be so utterly replaced by passion that each shade and contour seem to be the inside brought to light at its own urging, as sexuality is seen sometimes through swelling and congestion.

So—in short—color is consciousness itself, color is feeling, and shape is the distance color goes securely, as in our life we extend ourselves through neighborhoods and hunting grounds; while form in its turn is the relation of these inhabited spaces, in or out or up or down, and thrives on the difference between kitchen and pantry. This difference, with all its sameness, is yet another quality, alive in time like the stickiness of honey or the gently rough lap of the cat, for color is connection. The deeds and sufferings of light, as Goethe says, are ultimately song and celebration.

Praise is due blue, the preference of the bee.

But how many critics mimic Aristotle instead, although Aris-

[73]

totle's eyes were always in his reason: '. . . in painting: if someone should smear the picture with the most beautiful colors, but at random, he would not please us as much as if he gave us a simple outline on a white ground.' The Philosopher has his thumb on the scales. Which is more likely to hold our interest, he should have asked: beautiful colors laid on randomly, or any delicately graven scribble? because, to be fair, line should be matched against color, not color against outline. The unity of an outline is derivative anyway, borrowed from the object it presumably limns, and *that* unity may be quite imaginary. What unifies the shape of a typed 't' but function and familiarity? There is none in the mark itself. A color's unity is inherent, however, since it is continuously, insistently, indivisibly present in what it is. Furthermore, every color is a completed presence in the world, a recognizable being apart from any object, while a few odd lines (since a line is only an artificial edge), a few odd lines are: nothing —thin strings of hue . . . and what of that white ground Aristotle asks for? deny him that and give him a black base for a white design instead . . . then perhaps violet with green . . . chartreuse with red, so he can see how character comes and goes with color.

Well, we might march the halls of all the Old Schools and find few versions of these views. Winckelmann is as indifferent to quality as Kant. However, let us allow this statement of Berenson's, an echo with its echoes, to complete the case against color:

> It appears . . . as if form was the expression of a society where vitality and energy were severely controlled by mind, and as if colour was indulged in by communities where brain was subordinated to muscle. If these suppositions are true, we may cherish the hope that a marvelous outburst of colour is ahead of us.

In all the varieties of visual representation and reproduction of objects that are assumed to be outside ourselves, and of images flitting through our minds, colour must necessarily be the servant, first of shape and pattern, and then of tactile values and movement. Colour cannot range free but must serve rapid recognition and identification, facilitate the interpretation of shapes and the articulation of masses, and accelerate the perception of form, or tactile values, and movement. (*Aesthetics and History*)

Again and again we strike the same bigotry about blue, the same confusion of categories, the same errors of mind . . . and the same disastrous lapses of taste:

Pink and green horses may be tolerated in an *incunabulous* experimenter like Paolo Uccello, but I remember wincing at the sight of Impressionist portraits with faces and bosoms and hands blotched with vivid vegetable green reflected from the surrounding foliage, orange and scarlet from the sunshades held by the subjects. If the clearly expressed intention of Uccello, or Besnard, or Rolle, or Zorn had been to study the effect of reflections on horses' hides or women's skins, we should have adjusted ourselves accordingly. That was not the case. The portraits referred to will scarcely find now the admirers they had when their mere newness excited and, for an instant, fascinated the spectator. (*Aesthetics and History*)

$$* \quad * \quad *$$

Of the colors, blue and green have the greatest emotional range. Sad reds and melancholy yellows are difficult to turn up. Among the ancient elements, blue occurs everywhere: in ice and water, in the flame as purely as in the flower, overhead and inside caves, covering fruit and oozing out of clay. Although green enlivens the earth and mixes in the ocean, and we find it, copperish, in fire; green air, green skies, are rare. Gray and brown are widely distributed, but there are no joyful swatches of either, or any of exuberant black, sullen pink, or acquiescent orange. Blue is therefore most suitable as the color of interior life. Whether slick light sharp high bright thin quick sour new and cool or low deep sweet thick dark soft slow smooth heavy old and warm: blue moves easily among them all, and all profoundly qualify our states of feeling.

Kandinsky claims that a circle of yellow will seem to ooze from its center and even warmly approach us, while a similar circle of blue 'moves into itself, like a snail retreating into its shell, and draws away from the spectator. The eye feels stung by the first circle while it is absorbed into the second' (*Concerning the Spiritual in Art*).

Yellow cannot readily ingest gray. It clamors for white. But blue will swallow black like a bell swallows silence 'to echo a grief that is hardly human.' Because blue contracts, retreats, it is the color of transcendence, leading us away in pursuit of the infinite. From infra-red to ultra-violet, the long waves sink and the short waves rise. 'Just as orange is red brought nearer to humanity by yellow, so violet is red withdrawn from humanity by blue.'

When the trumpet brays, Kandinsky hears vermilion. The violin plays green on its placid middle string. Blues darken through the cello, double bass, and organ, for him, and the bassoon's moans are violet like certain kinds of gloom. He believes that orange can be rung from a steeple sometimes, while the joyous rapid jingle of the sleigh-bell reminds him of raspberry's light cool red. If color is one of the contents of the world as I have been encouraging someone—anyone—to claim, then nothing stands in the way of blue's being smelled or felt, eaten as well as heard. These comparisons are only slightly relative, only somewhat

[76]

subjective. No one is going to call the sounds of the triangle brown or accuse the tympanist of playing pink.

Some spices are true scarlets, I suppose, as pepper seems to be, and surely the richness of fine food often borders on brown. Earth tones appropriately rule the stove, and the carefully conceived kitchen will let porcelain and stainless steel stand for cleanliness, blue tile for planning and otherwise taking thought, while wood, clay, and copper, the mustards, reds, and deeper greens, signify the work itself, although one should notice that the grander a cuisine is the less robust its hues will be.

Still, we permit the appearance of our meats, sauces, fruits, and vegetables to dominate our tongues until it is difficult to divide a twist of lemon or a squeeze of lime from the colors of their rinds or separate yellow from its yolk or chocolate from the quenchless brown which seems to be the root, shoot, stalk, and bloom of it. Yet I hardly think the eggplant's taste is as purple as its skin. In fact, there are few flavors at the violet end, odors either, for the acrid smell of blue smoke is deceiving, as is the tooth of the plum, though there may be just a hint of blue in the higher sauces. Perceptions are always profound, associations deceiving. No watermelon tastes red. Apropos: while waiting for a bus once, I saw open down the arm of a midfat, midlife, freckled woman, suitcase tugging at her hand like a small boy needing to pee, a deep blue crack as wide as any in a Roquefort. Split like paper tearing. She said nothing. Stood. Blue bubbled up in the opening like tar. One thing is certain: a cool flute blue tastes like deep well water drunk from a cup.

That space in paper sacks which are too small to be re-used is blue. Sucking stones, too. Even if the sacks themselves are often tan and sandy, the stones are ovals of gray-blue granite. Molloy's sentences of calculation, so calm, so formed, so desperate, are blue to the pale core they contain, and at the bottom of the paper bags, as if waterlogged, there is always a little slip with the price of purchase. The pockets of the greatcoat and the pockets of the trousers, the tireless fist which is at itch to trade one for another, are blue like the empty sacks they resemble. There is a swim of blue in the toothbrush glass. The loneliness of clothes draped over the backs of chairs is blue; undies, empty lobbies, rumpled spreads are blue, especially when chenille and if orange; not body warmth or body smell or the acidulous salts of the vagina— no—blue belongs to the past—to the minutes after masturbation, to thought, to detachment and removal, fading, to the inside side of sex and the self that in the midst of pitch and toss has slipped away like a lucky penny fallen from a dresser.

IV

IMAGINE for a moment that I have gained possession of the famous talisman of Gyges, a ring (as Plato tells) which confers invisibility upon its wearer when the bezel's turned. Of course I can kiss, kill, and steal easily. Without paying, I can get in all the games. I can play tricks in a world of rubes. But what else?

My neighbors. I can spy: there's that buxom wench with the inviting eyes, and her husband, a stout, red-faced, and unappealing lout who wears, I've noticed, both a pair of suspenders and a belt. While they're hugging groceries from car to kitchen, I slip inside their house. I wish the ring eliminated sounds. They'll hear my breathing, and how my stiff clothes scrape. There she is, innocent and unaware, preparing salad at the sink.

Come. Walk through Blue Willow. There are pavilions, birds, green boughs like blue grapefruit, leaves like hanging lanterns, foliage like mascara'd eyes in midwink. I'm told it tells a story. And it may be the most popular pattern ever manufactured. Why? Stacks of them, fresh from Woolworth's, fill my neighbor's china closet. See the doves? When we twist the ring, we're in. There are peacock feathers, sunflowers blue in the face, ferny streamers, fuzzy puffs, each fastened above the blue wiggle of a streaked trunk, the ground beneath like a foamy wave. There are nowhere any normal shapes. It is in fact a land afloat on milk-white water. There are blue boats out, and best of all there is a bridge where three sages cross, island to island, carrying, as one makes it out, a shepherd's crook, a board or box, a string upon a handle. They know what it is: being blue; but who can feel how this world was once, counterfeiting has so changed it. Beyond the zagging fence a walk like a white shadow leads to wrinkled steps which have abruptly been unfolded from the portico of the great pagoda. We can see the inner windows, fanned and nowhere repetitious, then funny hatted houses in the distance, while the encircling calm of blue doodled borders—squares, scrolls, circles, diamonds, dots, checks, curls—drawn as if on the empty edge of the earth, keeps us lazily underneath the willow, by its water, the way the saucer which carries the pattern rests its cup.

She is still preparing salad at the sink.

Not very interesting.

What is fatso doing? reading the paper? My shoes squeak. I am too nervous to pay attention. What have they to say to one another?

Nothing.

Not very interesting.

I can't help holding my breath and soon I've all that forceful air to hiss. Why won't they quarrel, gossip, joke?

But suppose instead that suddenly I am scorched by a blue flame. I put my pain where the wound is and color where the flame is. Is this cleverness? My pain is not a detached affliction of the soul, and the philosopher, when he says the hurt's *in me*, should mean it's in my arm or elbow, because that's where *I* am, and in that area of air around me I call home.

If I've been bound by wires, and if I am now being burned with matches struck by my wife or some former friend or, worse, my son, the sorrow this causes me is another perception, although of a different kind: it is the realization of my relation to the world or at least to a part of it. The sorrow contains the flame, the pain, the revengeful person, disappointment about the past, guilt, horror, anger, awe, grief with regard to the future, fear, shame, plans for retribution, apprehension, pity, disbelief, pain again, and then once again, pain. My emotions may be mistaken sometimes, but each is the integration of a very complex and continually changing set of relations only temporarily stabilized this time in a blinding run of tears.

Thus, just as *seeing* blue involves a comparison between longer and shorter wavelengths over the total visual field, *being* blue consists of a set of comparisons too. And just as it is necessary for me to have the right visual equipment, good light and easy distance, an appropriately unpreoccupied mind, et cetera, simply to see in the most ordinary way, so I must be able to receive reports from all of my senses, estimate the character of my mental calculations, like Schopenhauer's genius, deepen toward the origin of every signal, shed prejudice, overcome any number of threatening neuroses, before my feelings, like my eyes, can be trusted; but this only means that feelings are much more complex than sensations by themselves (though by themselves they do not exist—what does?), and consequently that more—much more—can go wrong with them.

Furthermore, like those logical layers I touched upon earlier (blue the color, 'blue' the word, and Blue the Platonic Idea), our feelings have levels, and many are metapathetic. These logically remoter emotions are soon equal with the others (my desire for another man's wife commingles with the disgust I feel at my taste for flaccid boobs), and this new mix is felt afresh as still another feeling which, when the complete self is in fine fettle, with incredible immediacy and ease, disposes qualities correctly over the embattled Europe of my experience much as we crayoned countries in sixth-grade History in order to learn who had won what in the First World War: cleavage for the eye, martini on the tongue, heat to the head, aching in the belly, swelling within the prick, envy of the husband's proprietary arm now wrapped indecently under the heavy fall of her breasts, and contempt from the critical self shaken out like salt on everything. None of these inclusive responses is purely public, purely private; each of them is cognitive, the sum of whatever we know and are at any moment. We experience the world, balanced on our noses like the ball it is, turn securely through the thunder of our own applause.

But she is still preparing salad at the sink.

Why doesn't she slip out of those blue jeans and roll upon the floor in an agony of desire?

Because she is preparing salad at the sink.

And now I notice that there is an important element missing from my perception of her. Invisible, I can't see the faint fuzz of my cheeks or the framing fringe of my hair. Suppose, as I had wished a moment ago, I were inaudible. I should find, very quickly, how much I need to hear the sound of my own breathing. To hear the scene, but not myself: how odd . . . how horrible . . . how whimsical . . . how unnerving. Now I understand what a difference any kind of distance makes. How could I taste her lips and not taste my own, or run my hand upon her arm without its fingers being felt? Do I wish us both odorless in bed? (Fat persons, incidentally, are advised to wear blue. It will squeeze them in, as Kandinsky said, better than a corset. Have a plum.) The naked little girlfriend in the photo could not hear me, see me, either, and the woman I want undressed right now, this kitchen with its silly running water which I wish removed by lightning van, hubbie and paper wanded away to Nevernever Land, are stubbornly indifferent photographs which stare behind me like the polar bears.

Meanwhile I wait, releasing my breath beneath my shirt.

And meanwhile she continues to prepare salad at the sink.

Then it is not blue I see but myself seeing blue.

Perhaps I should come back at bedtime to watch them bathe in the dusk-blue light of the set, chew potato chips and other crunchies as they slowly sink . . . sag . . . settle like their pillows into grateful sleep.

No. I should go to a play. The characters will enter with their entrails already showing. No salads. Sinks. No squeaks. Whole lives will be compressed into a gesture . . . and then another. Or I should slip into a novel. My invisibility's complete. Unless I get caught in something like a Warhol movie, there won't be those long stretches watching people sleep. I can observe poor Portnoy beat his meat. And in fiction I can rub a ring which Gyges would have traded his to wear: one which painlessly permits a peek in any consciousness I care to.

The push toward blue in fiction has persisted from the beginning. It was immediately recognized that fiction could carry us, as the bride over the threshold, into domesticity. Suddenly there are sinks and sofas, hats and dresses, table manners. Intimacy. The movies have relieved this pressure somewhat, but writers remain unduly responsive to it. As readers, that's what we want: the penetration of privacy. We want to see under the skirt. And while we are peering at the page, though invisible to Prudence who is scratching her thigh, we are not invisible in fact—again an improvement over the ring which costs us the sight of ourselves. Words are one-way mirrors, and we can safely breathe, hoot, holler all we like to assure ourselves of our existence, and never once disturb Prudence easing her itch.

So at the sink, what is she *thinking*? Let her wash her greens, I go where it's blue . . . as blue as the Bloomsday book. 'Light sob of breath Bloom sighed on the silent bluehued flowers.' But she is thinking: tomorrow I have to remember to buy more salad oil. Frank likes the green kind with the white specks. It's on sale. And get some Woolite for the sheep.

Nonsense. I won't have it. She is thinking of her role as a woman in the world. She has a thing for the fellow next door. That's me. She is about to embark on an hour-long sexual fantasy during which time she'll petal up the radishes. We want to know. At once. Everything. And if it's going to be boring, we want the truth replaced by lies. Most novelists are bought. They will oblige. And even if our own neurotic natures prevent us from enjoying scenes of sodomy and fellatio, we will allow the hero time to ring a pencil with his teeth, or sit—ooo, aaaaah, tee-hee, oh boy, surprise!—upon a burr or pin or thumb or spike.

Books whose blueness penetrates the pages between their covers are books which, without depriving us of the comfort of our own commode or the sight of our liberal selves, place us inside a manufactured privacy. This privacy is really not that of someone else. It must be artificial because the real world plainly bores us. Impatient, we can't wait for nature to take its course. When we take our textual tour through the slums, we want crime, violence, starvation, disease, not hours of just sitting around. We want the world to be the world we read about in the papers: all news. What good is my ring if the couple I am using it to spy on make love in darkness once a month, and then are quick, inept, and silent? Better rob banks. The money is always there. What good is my peek at her pubic hair if I must also see the red lines made by her panties, the pimples on her rump, broken veins like the print of a lavender thumb, the stepped-on look of a day's-end muff? I've that at home. No. Vishnu is blue in all his depictions. Lord Krishna too. Yes. The blue we bathe in is the blue we breathe. The blue we breathe, I fear, is what we want from life and only find in fiction. For the voyeur, fiction is what's called *going all the way*.

The privacy which a book makes public is nevertheless made public very privately—not like the billboard which shouts at the street, or the movie whose image is so open we need darkness to cover the clad-ass and naked face that's settled in our seat. A fictional text enters consciousness so discreetly it is never seen outdoors . . . from house to house it travels like a whore . . . so even on a common carrier I can quite safely fill my thoughts with obscene adjectives and dirty verbs although the place I occupy is thigh-sided by a parson.

We like that.

Thus between the aesthetically irrelevant demands of the

[85]

reader and the aesthetically crippling personal worries of the writer, sexuality reaches literature as an *idée fixe*, an artifically sweetened distortion or an outright lie, while the literature itself leaks quality like a ruptured pipe.

This is not the same shade of blue Henry James had in mind when he invented Ralph Limbert, an author like himself who, as each book disappeared in a neglect as complete as the last tick of the clock, resiliently hoped for a popular success 'The Next Time.' Limbert is given the incorruptible artistry and felicitous bad luck always to aim for the mob and hit the few, choosing cheap subjects and enriching them as clay is, modeled into bronze, until in the twilight of his career, when there was to be no 'next time,' he accepted the plain inglorious and unromantic loneliness of the creative self. Then it seemed '. . . he had quite forgotten whether he generally sold or not. He had merely waked up one morning again in the country of the blue and had stayed there with good conscience and a great idea.'

Blue as you enter it disappears. Red never does that. Every article of air might look like cobalt if we got outside ourselves to see it. The country of the blue is clear.

*   *   *

It is not simple, not a matter for amateurs, making sentences sexual; it is not easy to structure the consciousness of the reader with the real thing, to use one wonder to speak of another, until in the place of the voyeur who reads we have fashioned the reader who sings; but the secret lies in seeing sentences as containers of consciousness, as constructions whose purpose it is to create conceptual perceptions—blue in every area and range:

[86]

emotion moving through the space of the imagination, the mind at gleeful hop and scotch, qualities, through the arrangement of relations, which seem alive within the limits they pale and redden like spanked cheeks, and thus the bodies, objects, happenings, they essentially define.

The condition I describe is not, as one might initially suppose, like that ascribed to Eva Flegen of Mörs, the Maid of Germany, who lived without meat on the smell of a rose, but, paradoxically, every loving act of definition reverses the retreat of attention to the word and returns it to the world. The landscape which emerges from the language which has made it is quite as lovely, vast and curious, as rich and prepossessing, as that of the deity who broke the silence of the void with speech so perfect the word 'tree' grew leaves and the syllables of 'sealion' swallowed fish.

The misleading miracle of the movies can nevertheless instruct us about prose. The silent film was full of magnificent action and exaggerated gestures as the actors strove to overcome the muteness of their medium. A Chaplin might occasionally manage, but most emotions cannot survive breast-beating. The talkie, on the other hand, while showing us how complicated thoughts and subtle feelings had been nearly snuffed out by the airless absence of speech, also demonstrated how cheap, thin, and stupid both became when the script was weak. Of course the camera fidgets in front of the speaking face. The telephone, a tire screech, the smash of glass, a ringing exchange of shots: these sounds issue from their images; but any conversation which rises above cliché like the first bird requires every photo in its neighborhood to be obedient and serve it. Fiction becomes visual by becoming verbal. The camera understands its enemy, and shuts its eye.

[87]

When Leo Feldman, Stanley Elkin's awesome merchant, enters his department store and is at once assailed by 'perfumes and facepowders, the mascaras, and polishes bright as sodas,' will *we* enter? only if his language enters us the way God's did Adam at whose bare word, as Sir Thomas Browne reminds us, 'were the rest of the creatures made.' Then the language fills the mouth as it was meant to. We feel the need to speak it. Accepting the words as our own, speaking the words as our own, we believe at last in their denotations. 'Art, art, thought Feldman, impresario of deep disks of rich rouge, pastel as flesh, of fine-grained dusting powders like soft, fantastic sand, of big plush puffs and cunning brushes.' This silent head-hummed sound we make is not a useless and annoying wail which has been wrenched by lack of oil from the machinery. When we hear 'big plush puffs' we do not have to see them, and 'deep disks of rich rouge' replace the feel of the tinted grease. Through the physical qualities of the language, Elkin moves his 'things' as if to music.

> He was obsessed by it, the merchandise laid out like a city, patterned, zoned as neighborhood, and missed nothing on the fluorescently tubed yellow wood and glass horseshoe counters. He knew without touching them the feel of the glass, greasy as plastic from the precious contact of shoppers, their leaned, open-palmed surrenders on the countertops, smudged from their groped investigations, their excited jabs at the glass: 'There, *there*—next to the white one.' (The counters, washed each night, bore a now intrinsic blur, ineffaceable as the cloud on an old watch crystal.) And could almost have told which belts had been sold from the tiers mounted like coiled snakes in their clear oblong boxes. And even which ties, perhaps, hanging thick as a curtain before some gay vaudeville. (Elkin: *A Bad Man*.)

Feldman's passion for his goods is instantly convincing because

Elkin's passion for the language which relates it is convincing. What the eye dwells on—loves—the ear hears. How often do we approach one another with the unashamed sensuality of Feldman approaching Men's Ready to Wear?

> Trailing his hand comfortlessly through the heaped, dark piles of socks, he looked out over the open rectangles of distant counters and cases and racks, and went toward Men's Ready to Wear to stand among the mountains of slacks, aware as always of the faint, sweet, oily smell of the massed cloth. He pulled at a rack of suits built into a wall, dollying it effortlessly forward on its big tracks, turning it soundlessly on its thick, greased shaft. He drew in one last deep lungful of the pleasant odor and moved on, the tweeds and herring-bones giving him, as he glanced at them in passing, a faint illusion of speed.

The sincere think it is enough to have stood by a stack of pants in a store one day and smelled something. We merely need remember Rupert Brooke's weak list of loved things, of which the rough male kiss of blankets is alone worthy of remark, to measure the distance here from cuff to crotch. Unfortunately we cannot follow Feldman the whole way down his legendary aisles, yet nothing but genre blindness could prevent us from seeing that there is no warmer, wealthier poetry being written in our time.

So to the wretched writer I should like to say that there's one body only whose request for your caresses is not vulgar, is not unchaste, untoward, or impolite: the body of your work itself; for you must remember that your attentions will not merely celebrate a beauty but create one; that yours is love that brings its own birth with it, just as Plato has declared, and that you should therefore give up the blue things of this world in favor of the words which say them: blue pencils, blue noses, blue movies, laws, blue legs and stockings, the language of birds, bees, and flowers as sung by longshoremen, that lead-like look the skin has when affected by cold, contusion, sickness, fear . . . chant and pray, since the day may begin badly, in a soggy light that moistens the soul before consciousness has cracked so every thought is damp as an anxious forehead, desire won't spark, and the morning prick is limp . . . consequently speak and praise, for the fall of the spirit, descending like a diver toward the floor of the ocean, is marked by increasing darkness, green giving way to navy, then a hair-wide range of hues which come to rest, among snowing fish and plants pale as paper, in a sightless night; and our lines are long when under water, loose and weedy, turning back upon themselves like the legs of a dying spider; we grow slack of feature in our melancholy, and the blue which marks the change is heavy, thick as ooze . . . so shout and celebrate before the shade conceals the window: blue bloods, balls, and bonnets, beards, coats, collars, chips, and cheese . . . while there is time and you are able, because when blue has left the edges of its objects as if the world were bleached of it, when the wide blue eye has shut down for the season, when there's nothing left but language . . . watered twilight, sour sea . . . don't find yourself clergy'd out of choir and chorus . . . sing and say . . . despite the belly ache and loneliness, new bumpled fat and flaking skin and drunkenness and helpless rage, despite dumps, mopes, Mondays, sheets like dirty plates, tomorrow falling toward you like a tower, lie in wait for that miraculous moment when in your mouth teeth turn into dragons and you do against the odds what Demosthenes did by the Aegean: shape pebbles into syllables and make

[90]

stones sound; thus cautioned and encouraged, commanded, warned, persist . . . even though the mattress where you mourn's been tipped and those corners where the nickels roll slide open like a slot to swallow them, clocks slow, and there's been perhaps a pouring rain, or factory smoke, an aging wind and winter air, and everything is gray.

This book was written for
all those who live in the
country of the blue
and is given in keeping
to Mary

St. Louis, September 13, 1975

ON BEING BLUE has been composed by Michael & Winifred Bixler. The typeface is Monotype Dante, designed by the archtypographer Giovanni Mardersteig, cut in its original version by the skilled punchcutter Charles Malin and first used in 1954. The mechanical recutting by The Monotype Corporation of this strong and elegant Renaissance design preserves the liveliness, personality, and dignity of the original. The third printing has been printed offset by Mercantile Printing Company on Warren's Olde Style and has been bound by New Hampshire Bindery.